Dbt

Mindfulness and Emotion Regulation Techniques

(Proven Psychological Techniques for Managing Trauma & Emotional Healing)

Roy Mendez

I0089824

Published By **Cathy Nedrow**

Roy Mendez

Dbt: Mindfulness and Emotion Regulation Techniques (Proven Psychological Techniques for Managing Trauma & Emotional Healing)

ISBN   978-1-7780063-5-7

No part of this guidebook shall be reproduced in any form without permission in writing from the publisher except in the case of brief quotations embodied in critical articles or reviews.

Legal & Disclaimer

The information contained in this book is not designed to replace or take the place of any form of medicine or professional medical advice. The information in this book has been provided for educational & entertainment purposes only.

The information contained in this book has been compiled from sources deemed reliable, and it is accurate to the best of the Author's knowledge; however, the Author cannot guarantee its accuracy and validity and cannot be held liable for any errors or omissions. Changes are periodically made to this book. You must consult your doctor or get professional medical advice before using any of the suggested remedies, techniques, or information in this book.

Table Of Contents

Table of...

Chapter 1: Navigate The Rollercoaster Ride

A young lady named Amelia resided in the bustling city of Veridian the city where towering skyscrapers cut through the skies and the streets vibrated with the sounds of the frantic footsteps. It was as if she were any individual walking around as she mingled with the rhythm of metropolitan pace. Yet, behind her calm facade was a rollercoaster of emotions waiting to wake up.

Amelia was taught to hide her feelings and hide them from the the world. However, as is often the case, life does have the ability to reveal secrets. An unintentionally came into contact with her in the busy train station on one tragic day. This caused her to misplace her damaged notebook. The pages slid open, revealing glimpses of poetry that moved and intimate insights. A smile of understanding, the man returned to her journal and wrote, "Embrace your emotions, for they are the gateway to your true self."

Amelia was struck by the words of a stranger and embarked for a journey to discover the inner workings of her emotions. The beginning chapter is a deep dive into her inner reflections, looking into the role of emotion in our lives. She explores the possibility of embracing our emotions, rather than burying them in our own minds, utilizing key ideas that come from the fields of philosophy, psychology and even personal experiences.

Amelia is able to demonstrate, with vivid narratives and vivid memories emotional states are not merely a source of irritation that should be ignored and are instead a set of compasses to help us navigate the maze of our lives. She shows the capability of being able to identify, understand the feelings of each that we experience, from joy to sadness.

Amelia weaves an exquisite emotional tapestry using rigorous analysis and beautiful words, defining their function and emphasizing their interconnectedness. Amelia reminds readers that by taking on the rollercoaster of emotions, you can develop a deeper understanding of themselves as well as establish crucial connections with other people.

The opening section, "The Awakening of Emotions," establishes the mood for a fascinating investigation of the human state of mind. The readers are invited on a rollercoaster of emotions, willing to take on the twists and turns of it with greater understanding and respect when they turn the pages. It all begins in the struggle of Amelia to accept her feelings, laying the foundation for the transformative chapters that follow.

UNDERSTANDING YOUR UNIQUE EMOTIONAL LANDSCAPE

They are the deep colors that shade the canvas of our lives. They pervade all aspects of the lives of people, affecting our thoughts, actions as well as our interpersonal relationships. Everyone has their own emotional terrain within ourselves an intricate landscape that is the key for personal development, self-discovery as well as positive interactions with other people. This piece will guide you through an engaging journey through how important it is to understand the emotional terrain you live in, and provide concrete insights as well as guidance to make the journey easy and informative.

Embracing the Emotional Spectrum:

They are not a binary entity and are part of a spectrum of human emotions. The emotional landscape of our lives is an intricate tapestry of experiences, similar to how the prism scatters light across various shades. Each emotion is unique and is unique and significance, ranging from joy of joy and love, to the deepest levels of sadness and fear. It's important to understand and accept the broad range of feelings we experience and realize that they're not evil or good however they are merely necessary signals which provide valuable insights to our own inner life.

Developing Self-Awareness:

Self-awareness training is essential to understand our personal emotional environment. It involves developing mindfulness and introspection so that we increase our awareness of the emotional experiences we experience. The first step is to discover the different levels of our dynamic world by paying close attention to the physical sensations and subtle signals of the flow and the flow of our feelings. A greater awareness can help us to be aware of and acknowledge the emotions we feel at any given moment, which allows us to develop a deeper knowledge of ourselves.

Uncovering the Sources of Your Emotions:

The emotional responses we experience aren't only isolated incidents, but instead are deeply rooted in the past. Understanding our emotional world involves examining and unravelling the roots of these reactions. It is possible to understand the root causes behind the emotional state of our being by considering about important experiences in our lives, childhood memories as well as relationships. This method allows us to link the dots to identify repeating patterns and determine the effect on our values, beliefs and influences from outside on the way we experience and deal with emotional states.

Emotional Intelligence Development:

Emotional intelligence refers to the ability to manage emotions and effectively express them. It is the process of developing empathy and compassion about the feelings of others and feelings, establishing deeper connections and enhancing our relations. It also involves the ability to control the emotions we experience, preventing the emotions from overpowering us or creating harm. You can find a healthier equilibrium between our emotional realm and our outer interactions with other people by honeing the skills.

Respecting Your Emotional Needs:

The care we give to the emotional health of our loved ones is vital to live a fulfilled life. It is about recognizing and embracing our needs for emotional well-being. Create a warm and welcoming environment that encourages emotional growth and resilience through focusing on self-care and self-love. Setting appropriate boundaries is crucial in ensuring our emotional safety and addressing our desires. In addition, asking for assistance from family, friends or professionals when you need it helps in navigating the emotional landscape with clarity and perception.

Accepting Change and Resilience:

The dynamic world around us isn't an object that is static, it is a opportunity for personal development and acceptance of oneself. It is possible to openly be ourselves and freely share our thoughts through embracing vulnerability as an asset and establishing deeper bonds to others. It is possible to build authentic relationships and be able to engage in genuine conversations since we're open.

Additionally, recognizing your emotions as catalysts to improvement and learning lets us adjust to change, grow, and even recover from the failures. Resilience develops by overcoming challenges, adapting to change and taking pleasure in our emotional development.

Embracing The Power Of Your Emotions As A Catalyst For Growth

The world of our emotions holds a wealth of strength and wisdom in every one of us. The emotions we experience, frequently ignored or ignored can be used to be catalysts for individual growth and improvement. In a society that prefers reason and logic It is crucial to be aware of the transformative potential of our feelings and discover how to use the power of our emotions to grow. In this article we'll explore how important it is to embrace your emotions, and the ways they could be used as an inspiration in our quest for self-discovery as well as the personal development.

How Well Do You Know The Function of Emotions?

The emotions we experience aren't simply random fluctuations that occur in our lives. they are inextricably linked to our beliefs, thoughts and experience. Every emotion sends out a specific message, and each has its own purpose. For example, fear may signal imminent danger while joy could provide moments of joy and satisfaction. Knowing the significance of our emotions can allow us to gain insight into our own and the world around us.

Identifying Emotional Intelligence:

The ability to analyze, perceive and regulate one's own feelings as well as to be able to identify and feel empathy for those of other people. Self-awareness and self-regulation, empathy, and a successful set of interpersonal abilities are all a part of this.

Our ability to manage our emotional surroundings better, make more informed judgements, and make important connections by gaining emotional wisdom.

Embracing Emotional Intelligence:

The basis of harnessing the ability of our emotions is an awareness of our emotions. It involves gaining a deep understanding of our emotions in addition to recognizing the subtle distinctions and patterns in our own. Awareness of emotions can help us identify emotions, triggers, and themes that are recurring, giving important insights into our most fundamental objectives and desires.

Changing Emotional Triggers:

The triggers for emotional reactions are those that trigger us to experience major emotional responses. They may be a consequence of previous experiences, conflicts that are not resolved, or deeply established opinions. Instead of trying to avoid or suppress these triggers, it is possible to take them as an opportunity to grow personally. It is possible to heal the scars of past traumas or confront beliefs that limit us, and increase our capacity for emotional growth by examining the causes of the triggers.

Acceptance of Vulnerability and Authenticity:

The emotions, as they are defined, are fragile reflections of our self-images. You must accept the vulnerable and genuine side to gain the power of emotions. It means letting ourselves be heard and seen, and also expressing our feelings without worry of being judged and disqualified. This allows us to develop deeper relationships with other people, promote trust, and establish the space to allow for growth in our emotional state by embracing our vulnerability.

Developing Emotional Resilience:

Resilience in the emotional realm is the capacity to adjust and recover from challenges. It allows us to confront challenges, setbacks and emotional stress with a sense of grace and determination. It helps us build resilience through the process of learning from our experience by finding meaning and purpose in difficult situations, and utilizing your emotions as fuel to drive personal growth if we accept the strength of our feelings.

Chapter 2: Building Personalized Strategies

The journey of life is that is filled with many events that range from great to tough. It is a journey through which we face difficulties, challenges, and traverse periods of uncertainty on the way. Our innate abilities allow us to draw on our coping powers, unique strategies that allow us to develop resilience and be successful when faced with challenges, and to manage these ups and downs.

In this book that is comprehensive we'll explore different strategies to cope as well as assist you in devising your own strategies for managing stress and to deal with life's difficulties and trials.

We gain the understanding and knowledge needed to make shrewd choices and build a customized tools for resilience through thoroughly being aware of the many strategies for coping readily available.

Issue-Focused Coping:

Problem-focused coping can be described as a form of coping. It involves taking actions to tackle the underlying cause behind the problem. This strategy is most effective when faced with real-world issues or situations that require an active approach to problem solving. The approach of focusing on the problem allows us to take a proactive approach by analyzing the circumstances, gathering information in the form of innovative ideas, and implementing strategies. In focusing our attention to find effective solutions and solutions, we can have a stronger confidence in our abilities and more prepared for challenging circumstances.

Emotion-Focused Coping:

In contrast to addressing outside circumstances, emotional-focused coping concentrates on controlling the emotional effects of an event. It is about recognizing the emotions we feel, and communicating them in a healthy manner as well as seeking assistance from friends and family as well as engaging in self-care practices. In the event of unpredictability or stressful situations emotional coping is a way to help you manage your emotions as well as build up our inner strength and attain emotional balance. This approach allows us to deal with our emotions and build resilience in the confronting of difficulties.

Cognitive Restructuring:

It is a method of coping that involves challenging and revising our beliefs and thoughts regarding a situation. The goal is to change false or negative thinking patterns by better, more believable and positive thoughts. It is possible to develop an optimistic mindset which decreases stress levels, increases the ability to solve problems, and increases the resilience of our bodies by questioning the beliefs that we have about ourselves. Cognitive restructuring helps us with creating a more balanced and more confident perspective. It allows people to tackle challenges more confidently and with greater flexibility.

Social Support:

Getting help, guidance, and understanding from other individuals is a crucial way of coping. Humans are social beings and our interactions with people have a major impact on our general well-being. Social support may be in a variety of ways, such as confiding in a trusted family member or a family member participating in support group, or seeking expert counsel from counselors or therapists.

sharing our thoughts, feelings and experience with people is not just the feeling of being part of something bigger as well as provides vital knowledge, compassion and support. Through the development of relationships and keeping an emotional support system, social help helps us recognize that we're not the only ones when we face challenges, and increases the resilience of our lives.

Self-Care:

Being in a state of physical, emotional and mental wellbeing is a matter of practicing self-care. This means putting in place a plan of action as well as behaviors that nourish and refuel our bodies and minds. Self-care can help us replenish our reserves of energy, ease tension, and boost our ability to cope. Regular exercising, mindfulness or meditation as well as engaging in artistic outlets, or simply being in the outdoors are just a few ways to take care of yourself. having enough sleep and rest as well as practicing relaxation techniques, feeding our bodies healthy diet, and setting limits in order to ensure our wellbeing. Self-care is essential to maintain the balance and resilience of our lives and is not something we can afford to do as a luxury.

Creating Individualized Coping Strategies:

Self-Reflection and Self-Awareness:

The first step towards developing customized coping strategies is self-reflection and awareness of oneself. Spend time to research and identify your strengths, interests, and values. desires. Reminisce about your experiences in the past and discover coping strategies that worked before for your. Which activities or routines bring you peace of mind, calm and an overall sense of wellbeing? Knowing your tendencies and patterns can help you select the most appropriate strategies to meet your needs and needs.

Experimentation and Learning:

There's no standard strategy for coping. It is essential to play around using a variety of coping methods and evaluate their effects on the overall wellbeing of your body. Try out problem-focused, emotional-focused mental restructuring, social support and self-care actions. Be aware of how each approach affects your thoughts, feelings and overall mental health. Keep an open mind and open to changing and adjust your strategy according to what is most effective for you in different situations.

Create a Coping Toolbox:

In order to develop coping strategies that are unique make a toolbox for coping - a assortment of a variety of strategies and methods that you could draw your own in various circumstances. This toolkit is an aid to assist you build resilience and overall well-being. Incorporate deep breathing and writing exercises, taking part with creative activities, doing mindfulness or meditation, gaining the right social network, and engaging physically, and receiving help from professionals if required. A variety of coping techniques available will ensure that you're ready to tackle any obstacle that might arise.

Consistency and Adaptability:

If you want to be resilient the need for consistency is vital. Create strategies to cope with stress as a regular element of your routine even when all is good. The practice of coping regularly improves your capabilities and the ability to deal with challenging scenarios. While you're at it, be flexible and ready to alter the strategies you employ to cope. The world is constantly changing and the circumstances change. The ability to adapt your methods of coping will allow you to successfully face challenges that are new and increase your endurance.

Remember to exercise self-compassion in all your ways of coping. Accept that the process of coping doesn't necessarily require perfectionism or all the solutions. The key is accepting who you are and being kind to yourself as well as accepting that disappointments as well as tough feelings are normal in the human experience. When you encounter challenges take care to be patient, kind and understanding of your self. Self-compassion helps build resilience and allows you to learn and grow through every challenge.

Chapter 3: Cultivating A Toolbox Of Effective

The journey of life is filled with ups and downs as well as triumphs, struggles, and challenges. It is inevitable that we will encounter hardship as well as unexpected obstacles on the way. Strategies for coping serve as an defense, offering us the resources we require to conquer these obstacles and ensure our overall wellbeing. There are many different ways to cope can be considered equally. Every person is different, having their own unique needs as well as preferences and capabilities. In this post we'll discuss how important it is to create tools for effective strategies for coping that can be tailored to meet your specific requirements, which will help you build resilience, reduce anxiety, and promote wellbeing.

What Are Coping Mechanisms?

Strategies for coping are deliberate actions and strategies we employ to deal with stress, control our moods and emotions, as well as deal with difficult scenarios. They're essential to achieve peace, improving mental wellbeing, and building resilience. You can choose and develop the right toolkit for us that meets our needs, through learning about the many ways of coping readily available.

Active Coping Strategies:

The goal is to take proactive steps that directly target the cause of the stress or adverse situation. This approach allows individuals to confront issues in a timely manner and regain control. Finding solutions, seeking assistance or advice, creating strategies, and then taking actions to resolve the issue are instances of active coping strategies. It is possible to develop a proactive attitude as well as build up resilience. We enhance our capability to manage challenges by utilizing effective coping techniques.

Emotion-Focused Coping Methods:

Strategies for coping that are focused on methods focussed on in regulating and managing the emotional responses to events. These strategies are extremely helpful when we're not able to manage the situation or have to deal with strong emotional reactions. Relaxation techniques, mindfulness and seeking out social support writing, and participating in things that provide happiness and peace are just a few ways to cope with emotion. Strategies for coping with emotions help us to recognize and managing our feelings as well as enhancing our resilience and wellbeing.

Cognitive strategies for coping:

It involves changing our mindsets and perceptions in order to create healthy and flexible reactions to stress. These strategies concentrate on the way we perceive and perceive events, aiding our minds in redefining negative thought habits and establishing a more positive outlook. In challenging negative thinking, focusing on gratitude and positive self-talk as well as reframing events from an optimistic perspective are just some ways to improve cognitive coping. It is possible to improve our capacity to handle problems, lessen anxiety, and improve wellbeing by developing the ability to cope with stress in a cognitive manner.

Self-Care Coping Strategies:

Strategies for self-care and coping are focused on keeping our bodies emotional and mental health. It involves actively engaging in self-care activities as well as relaxation and renewal. Strategies for self-care and coping include exercise regularly as well as mindfulness and meditation and adequate rest, healthy eating habits, setting limits for hobbies and creativity as well as prioritizing the things that bring satisfaction and joy. Self-care coping skills is essential for ensuring general well-being as well as replenishing resources for energy.

DEVELOP MINDFULNESS PRACTICES TO RIDE OUT YOUR INTENSE EMOTIONS

They are an integral component of our human experiences. They enhance our lives and provide valuable insights and allow us to connect with our authentic selves. But, intense emotions can be overwhelming and challenging to deal with at times.

The techniques of mindfulness can help you deal with these emotions better and develop feelings of emotional wellbeing. In this post we'll explore the ways that developing mindfulness skills will help you manage emotional turmoil. The article will examine the transformative effects of mindfulness, provide ways to incorporate mindfulness into the daily routine and guide you along an emotional resilience path.

Mindfulness in Action:

Mindfulness refers to focusing our attention on the present moment mindfully in a state that is full of curiosity and detachment. It involves examining thoughts or emotions as well as body experiences without getting lost in the moment or reacting in a rash manner.

You develop a more profound consciousness of the inner experiences we experience as well as the capacity to respond to them more effectively and with compassion by practicing mindfulness.

THE ADVANTAGES OF MINDFULNESS IN DEALING WITH STRONG EMOTIONS:

Increased Emotional Awareness:

The practice of mindfulness helps us to become more mindful of our feelings. It helps us gain an understanding on the causes, habits and the underlying reasons behind the powerful emotions we experience by observing the emotions without judgement. A greater awareness of emotions enables us to react to our feelings in a more thoughtful and efficient manner.

Optional Regulation:

Through regular mindfulness and regularly, we will improve the ability of our bodies to manage strong emotions. The practice creates a space which allows us to react instead of reacting impulsively, through cultivating a non-reactive mindset to our emotions. Mindfulness allows us to distinguish between the eruption of intense emotions and our subsequent actions, which allows us to determine how to act.

Improved Emotional Resilience:

It builds resilience to emotional stress which allows us to bounce back from emotional trauma. It provides us with the tools that we require to navigate the ocean of intense feelings without becoming lost. The ability is gained to be able to remain in the space of our feelings, acknowledge the ephemeral nature of them, and develop a sense peace and stability through meditation.

Create Mindfulness Trainings to deal with Emotions that are Strong:

Mindful Breathing :

It is among the simplest and accessible meditation exercises. Take a few minutes each day, concentrating on the feeling of your breath flowing into out. Pay attention to your abdomen's rising and falling, or the feeling of air flowing through your nostrils. If your thoughts wander back to your breath, without judgement or criticism.

Body Scan Meditation:

You can try a body scan practice to be more conscious of the physical feelings associated to intense emotions. Starting at the upper part of your head, focus your attention on every part of your body and observe any aches, pains, or physical sensations that appear. Relax your mind upon these feelings without trying to alter them. Instead just acknowledge the presence of them.

Emotion Labeling:

If strong feelings arise be sure to label them with no judgment. Tell yourself "This is my anger," "This is my sadness," or "This is my fear." The act of labeling your emotion can create an illusion of distance that allows you to look at it in a neutral way instead of being entrapped in its grasp. It creates a sense space while also reducing the possibility for reactive actions.

Loving-Kindness Meditation:

By practicing loving-kindness meditation, one will develop compassion and kindness towards yourself and other people. Relax and repeat words such as "May I be safe, happy, healthy, and able to live with ease." Send your very best wishes to family members as well as acquaintances and people with whom you not agree. This can help improve your emotional health and strengthens connections by cultivating empathy, understanding as well as forgiveness.

Make time for thought-provoking journaling, where you are able to explore and share your feelings without judgement. Let the words effortlessly flow onto your pages while you write down your experience, thoughts and emotions. This process allows for self-expression in self-expression, self-discovery, as well as insights into your personal environment.

Integration of Daily Life:

Expand your mindfulness beyond the realms of formal practices and incorporate it into your day life. Participate in every day activities like eating, walking or talking with a conscious mind. Keep track of any sensations thoughts, feelings, or ideas which arise during these moments. Incorporating mindfulness into your everyday routine and routines, you can open yourself towards greater awareness and presence.

Seek Guidance and Community:

Consider joining a mindfulness group, participating in workshops or consulting with an experienced mindfulness instructor. These methods can give you guidance, encouragement as well as a feeling of belonging while you build your practice of mindfulness. Being connected to others who are in a similar journey can provide both a positive and uplifting experience.

Patience and Self-Compassion:

It's important to understand that gaining mindfulness takes some time and perseverance. Give yourself a hug and develop a more compassionate perspective. Be aware that your attention can wander, or your intense feelings can be overwhelmed sometimes. Instead of being critical try to treat the times you are experiencing with compassion and openness to re-starting.

AWARENESSING THE POWER OF YOUR breath to find calm in the midst of the turmoil Finding moments of peace and peace in our hectic and frequently chaotic surroundings could be a treat. Breath, on the other hand, can be an extremely powerful tool that is available whenever we need to assist to navigate through the trials of our lives with ease and peace.

Simply focusing your attention on the breath can help us return to our present as well as instill a sense of calm and allow for inner peace. in this course. We will discuss the profound effects of mindful breathing. explore various breathing methods as well as accompany your journey in using the power of breathing to find peace in turbulent times with this comprehensive article.

The Science of Breathing and Calm:

Breathing is an essential biochemical process that we ignore. Yet, deliberate breathing can be a major influence on the physical, mental as well as emotional conditions. When we're feeling overwhelmed, stressed, or feeling overwhelmed, our breathing is sluggish and shallow which is a sign of the fight or flight response within the body. Our body triggers the relaxation mechanism by intentionally breathing slower and deeper and triggering a series of bodily changes which create an impression of calm and wellbeing.

The Advantages of Conscious Breathing:

Stress Reduction:

The practice of mindful breathing has been proven to lower the levels of cortisol as well as stress hormones and physical signs of stress. You can create a sense of peace and calm when we engage in concentrated breathing, which allows our bodies to deal with stressful situations in a more relaxed manner.

Emotional Control:

Our breath is inextricably connected to our emotional state. It is possible to be aware of our mood and control the emotions we experience by paying attention to the breath. The practice of mindful breathing can assist us to deal with extreme emotions such as fear, anger, sadness. In addition, it can allow for emotional equilibrium and strength.

The act of breathing with awareness has a profound effect on our mood. The mind is calmed and create a state that is present by focusing on the breath. This helps improve our ability to concentrate, make informed decisions and handle situations with focus and confidence.

Increases Oxygenation and Blood Flow:

A deep and deliberate breathing pattern boosts oxygenation and blood flow improving overall health and well-being. The ability to breathe can boost the capacity of your lungs, breathing and immune system functioning and overall cardiovascular overall health. The body is nurtured on a cellular level through using the power of breath. This can boost energy levels and the longevity of our lives.

Calming Breathing Techniques:

Diaphragmatic breathing is often referred to as deep breathing or belly breathing, is the process of completely activating your diaphragm. Place one hand on your stomach, and the other on your chest. Inhale deeply through your nose. Feel your abdomen rise. Then gently exhale from the mouth, being aware of your stomach sinking. Take a few minutes to practice this practice, with your eyes focusing on the gradual rising and falling of your stomach.

The Box Breathing is a practice which involves equilibrating the length of your breath by holding your breath and then exhaling, then continuing the breathing procedure. Inhale deeply for four seconds then hold the breath for 4 counts and exhale after four seconds and then breathe repeatedly for four times. Repeat the process several times to maintain a consistent and constant rhythm.

Breathing into only one nostril at time is known as breathe through both nostrils. Take a deep breath through your left nostril as you place your right hand across the right nostril. Next, with your ring finger to seal the left nostril. Exhale through the right nostril. Breathe through your right nostril, then close it using your thumb and exhale from the left nostril. Repeat the pattern in alternating fashion many times while focusing on breathing in a calm, steady manner through the nostrils.

4-7-8 Breathing: This breathing method is a relaxing breathing practice. It involves inhaling for four count and holding for seven minutes, before slowly exhaling for 8 count. The pattern helps regulate the breath and creates a deep state of calm. Repeating this pattern will help your mind and body to fall into the state of calm.

The practice of mindful breathing: Mindful breathing can be the easiest and most practicable breathing technique. Relax in a relaxed posture and pay attention to the feeling of your breath. Pay attention to your cool exhale and warmth of your exhale. Maintain your regular breathing pattern by observing it, without judgement or the desire to alter the rhythm. If you find your mind wandering to other places, slowly bring it back to your breath, allowing you to completely be in the present time.

Including Breathwork in Your Daily Life:

Making use of your breath's potential is more than just a few strategies. The key is to develop an organized and disciplined approach to your breathing throughout your day routine. Here are some suggestions to incorporate breathing exercises in your routine

Morning Ritual: Kick off your day by taking a few minutes of focusing breathing. Make time for practicing your breathing style of choice and set a relaxing and calm tone for your coming day.

Pause for a few minutes throughout your day, to keep track on your breathing. Pause for a moment to take a breath, shut your eyes as much as you can and then take a few slow and slow breathes. It helps you relax and concentrate your thoughts through resetting the neurological system.

Focus Your Attention on Your Breath During Stressful Events In the event of difficult or stressful situations, pay focus to your breathing. Be aware of any tension or weak breathing, and then deliberately increase and slow down your breathing. This allows you to take on the challenge with more focus and calm.

Nighttime Wind-Down: Prior to going to bed, do some relaxation breathing exercises to ease your mind and get ready for bed. Deep, slow breaths with concentration on relaxation will enable you to unwind and get a great restful night.

Utilize breathing to serve as a anchor throughout the day to help bring you back into the actual time. Inhale slowly anytime you feel disoriented or overwhelmed. Allow yourself to connect with your present and present.

Chapter 4: Manage Your Anger And Frustration

Frustration and anger are common emotions that we experience at times. But they could create havoc in the quality of our relationships, wellbeing, as well as our overall wellbeing If they are not controlled. The ability to control the anger and frustration we feel can be a transformational procedure that lets us gain control of our emotions, create better relationships, and improve wellbeing in our emotions. In this article we'll look at different strategies and ways of controlling the inner fire and channeling emotions effectively while finding tranquility amid the chaos of anger and rage.

A Point of View on Anger and Frustration:

Anger is a reaction to emotion which occurs when we feel an unfairness, threat or anger. The emotion can manifest in an explosion of energies, which is accompanied by physical feelings, thoughts that are racing, as well as a desire to act recklessly. Recognizing the triggers behind it and the patterns of anger are the first step towards managing anger successfully.

The effects of frustration: The cause of frustration is usually obstacles, expectations that are not met or difficulties. The result can be feelings of despair, anger as well as stress accumulate. Being aware of the role that frustration plays in our psychological landscape is essential to develop efficient strategies for coping.

ANGER AND FRUSTRATION MANAGEMENT TECHNIQUES:

Know Yourself:

Be aware of yourself by paying attention to your body and feelings when you're angry or frustrated. Be aware of your bodily emotions, feelings as well as triggers that are to these feelings. The awareness allows you to stop the anger before it grows and allows you to choose an appropriate response.

Have A Deep Breathing Exercise:

In order to trigger your body's relaxation reaction, do deeply breathing exercises and methods of relaxation. Relax and breathe deeply whenever you're angry or annoyed, and focus on the feeling of breath moving through your body and out. For calming your mind and ease tension, try combining this exercise with a progressive relaxation of your muscles as well as visualization and meditation.

Expressive Writing:

Writing can be a great therapy outlet that lets you vent and deal with your frustration and frustration. Write down your thoughts, feelings, and experience. This helps with an effective externalization of your emotions as well as gaining perspective and the release of anger.

Cognitive Restructuring:

It's the process of breaking and altering destructive cognitive patterns that trigger the anger and irritation. Be aware of and change illogical ideas or mental distortions that are causing you to be angry, like the all-or-nothing mentality or personalization, by using better-balanced and more real notions. Cognitive restructuring makes it possible to see things in a variety of ways and to respond in a more rational and objective manner.

Aggressive Communication:

Learn to communicate effectively and communicate your needs, limits and anger in a respectful and effectively. Develop the ability to communicate effectively as well as listen carefully and work out mutually beneficial solutions. It is possible to avoid the bottled up feelings and reduce the risk of having explosive episodes of anger through assertive communication.

Emotional Regulation and Mindfulness:

Engage in mindfulness practices to develop conscious awareness in the present and non-judgmental acceptance of your feelings. If you are annoyed or angry, take note of the sensations, thoughts and impulses, and do not react. The practice of mindfulness allows you to stop and choose a calm action, and stay clear of impulse-driven reactions that are fueled by anger.

Healthy Coping Techniques:

Employ healthy strategies for coping with stress to effectively manage your frustration and anger. Boxing or running, for instance, can help in easing tension and anxiety. Music, painting, or writing poetry are options that let individuals to express their thoughts. Discover activities that leave you feel peaceful, happy and content.

Seeking Help:

In the event that anger and frustration become overwhelming, turn to trusted family members, friends or professionals for assistance. Discuss your feelings and thoughts or seek out advice and try out coping strategies using the support of others. Chatting with someone who is able to provide a sympathetic ear and perspectives can be helpful in easing tension and anger.

Time-Outs:

If your frustration or anger is at a peak you should take a break to escape the trigger incident. Choose a peaceful place to think about your feelings and practice calm techniques as well as engage in self-care. You could do this by taking an outing in the fresh air or listening to relaxing music, relaxing in a hot bath or participating in a fun activity.

Take a look at seeking out professional assistance If your frustration and anger remain and exert a significant impact on your daily life. Counselors or therapists can assist you in identifying the root causes of your anger, help you learn different strategies for dealing with anger as well as provide you with a secure setting for emotional healing and improvement.

Creating a Long-Term Strategy:

Controlling the emotions of anger and frustration is an ongoing task that demands perseverance, self-reflection and commitment. Think about creating a strategy for the long term to help you along the way:

Include regular routines that enhance the quality of your life, including journaling, mindfulness meditation or relaxing exercises. It is crucial to be consistent in developing new habits and building the ability to endure.

Support Network: Connect with those who can understand and appreciate your struggles. Look for help groups, online forums or even workshops in which you are able to connect with people that are experiencing similar feelings.

Self-Compassion: All along your journey do self-compassion and self forgiveness. Be aware that handling anger and anger is not easy and setbacks are likely to be inevitable. Be open to growth and development by taking care of yourself and respect.

Continuous Learning: Discover the management of anger, emotional regulation and skills for resolving conflicts. Take a class, read books or download podcasts that provide useful suggestions and methods.

The transformation of anger into assertiveness and positive actions

Anger can be a powerful emotion that, if it is not controlled properly, could be harmful to the health of our loved ones and also affect our relationship. However, anger, on however, can become the catalyst to positive transformation as well as assertiveness and positive actions if handled correctly. In this comprehensive article we'll look at the most effective methods and strategies that harness the power of anger and channeling the anger into assertiveness and redirecting it towards positive results. The goal is to establish more positive connections, be more assertive and create a positive change in your life and people around you through mastering the art in converting anger.

Recognizing Your Anger:

Accept and acknowledge your anger First step to changing the way you feel about anger is to acknowledge and accept the existence of it. Be aware that anger is a normal emotion that can be triggered through perceived dangers, injustices or even disappointments. The way to make room to grow and change through acknowledging the rage you feel with no judgment.

Recognize triggers and patterns: Find out the exact triggers and patterns that can lead to anger. Are you referring to a particular situation or behavior? Recognizing your triggers helps you to be more aware and control your anger.

USING ANGER TO EFFECT POSITIVE CHANGE

Take a moment to reflect and pause: If you begin to feel angry it is a good idea to take time to ponder. Avoid reacting rashly. Think about what's behind the anger. Do you feel any deep emotion of fear, hurt or anger? It will enable you to gain insight into the underlying emotional feelings driving the rage.

Exercise skills to manage your emotions during the midst of a moment. Relaxation techniques, deep breathing and progressive relaxation of muscles as well as visualization techniques will assist in relaxing your mind and body to react sensibly instead of reactively.

Anger can be a powerful resource of energy that could be used to create positive actions. Instead of letting it spiral out of control and become destructive, channel that energy towards positive activities. Participate in activities that are aligned with your ideals and bring about positive changes, like exercising, artistic endeavors as well as advocacy.

Assertiveness Training:

Determine Your Boundaries and Needs Be aware of your wants and needs, then establish clearly defined limits. Insistency is based on an awareness of oneself. If you're aware of your goals and the acceptable for your self, you will be able to effectively convey your message.

Effective communication is vital to turning anger into action. Communicate your thoughts, feelings and personal boundaries in a clear and respectful manner. Utilize "I" expressions to express your opinion without accusing or critiquing.

Active Listening: Make use of active listening to gain a better understanding of the viewpoints of other people. Engage with others in a healthy way and uncover the common ground of others by listening to their concerns.

In the event of a conflict it is best to seek resolution through transparent and candid conversation. Instead of seeking to "win" the dispute, focus on finding an acceptable solution that is mutually beneficial. Look at compromises and working together for positive outcomes.

Get help and develop your skills If assertiveness seems to be a struggle for you, get advice and assistance. Take part in training for assertiveness or talk to an therapist to develop your skills in communicating and increase confidence in your ability to express your concerns.

KEEPING LONG-TERM TRANSFORMATION ALIVE

A regular self-reflection as well as self-care helps keep you in tune with your feelings and the progress you've made. Activities for self-care that feed your body, mind, and soul will make improve your overall health.

Make the most of your mistakes Transformation is a process, and mistakes are inevitable. Take the lessons learned from your mistakes as well as stumbles, and then turn these into opportunities to grow and improvement in your self.

Be patient and persistent Take patience and perseverance to alter habits that are deeply embedded. Keep yourself in good spirits when you are working to transform the anger you feel into confidence. Recognize small successes and stay committed to the growth you are achieving.

Chapter 5: Shifting Negative Self-Talk

The inner conversations we have, commonly known as self-talk has an impact on self-esteem, optimism, and general wellbeing. Self-talk that is negative, such as the self-defeating, self-sabotaging beliefs that are negative and thoughts, may hinder your personal growth and bring joy to our lives.

But, we will increase self-confidence, build self-esteem, and develop an optimistic and positive mental attitude by deliberately rewiring our internal dialogue. In this article we'll look at ways to identify ways to transform negative self-talk to positive and encouraging conversations within ourselves. It is possible to cultivate a positive and empowering mindset that drives you to success and satisfaction through mastering the art changing your inner dialog.

Negative Self-Talk Awareness:

The first step to change negative self-talk is becoming conscious of the negative self-talk. Take note of your thoughts when they come up in the course of your day. Note any pattern that are self-critical, self-doubt or self-limiting belief patterns. Change and challenge the negative thoughts patterns you have if you recognize them.

Negative Self-Talk Types:

Self-talk that is negative can come in a variety of varieties, such as self-criticism, comparison, catastrophizing and the imposter syndrome. Be aware of the specific types of self-talk that you engage in, so you are able to tackle them with greater effectiveness.

HOW TO REWRITE YOUR INNER DIALOGUE

Challenge Negative Thoughts:

After you've discovered self-talk that is negative Consider examining its legitimacy. Think about whether your thoughts stem from facts or if they are based on false beliefs. Reframe negative thinking with more positive and realistic ones. In other words Instead of thinking "I always mess up," change it to "I am capable of learning from my mistakes and improving."

Self-Compassion:

Be kind and patient with your self. Self-examination should replace the role of self-criticism. Be the same person you would treat a acquaintance in the same situation. Be aware of your shortcomings and realize the fact that mistakes are an essential element of learning.

Positive Affirmations:

Utilize positive affirmations to fight negative self-talk. Make affirmations that are positive to you, and are a representation of the traits you want to develop. Keep repeating these affirmations regularly in particular during times where you are feeling doubt or negative. "I am deserving of love and success," "I believe in my ability to overcome obstacles," and "I am deserving of happiness and fulfillment" These are just a few instances.

Be surrounded by positive influences including supportive family members or mentors as well as positive facts. Engage in events which inspire and encourage you. Limit your exposure to negative circumstances and those that contribute to self-talk negativity.

Gratitude Practice:

Create a practice of gratitude in order to focus your mind on positive events in your life. Appreciating and acknowledging your strengths and achievements allows the mind to change its perspective and helps you develop a positive perspective.

Set Realistic Ambitions:

Break down larger goals into manageable, smaller projects. Create realistic goals to yourself and appreciate every step of the way. Be aware that success takes the time and energy of a professional and that mistakes are an opportunity to grow and not excuses for being critical of your self.

Taking on Long-Term Transformation:

The art of rewriting your own inner dialog is a continuous procedure that requires both persistence and perseverance. Take care of yourself when you learn to break old thinking patterns, and then substitute them for new and more effective ones. If you experience failures, develop self-compassion and focus at the achievements you've made to date.

Journaling: Write down your thoughts and feelings in a notebook for recording your thoughts and feelings. thoughts. Make use of it to uncover the negative habits of self-talk and to explore different perspectives. Write down your good things, accomplishments and happy occasions. Write down your journal entries often to keep track of your growth and encourage positive self-talk.

Cognitive restructuring exercises can be employed to address and change the way you view negative thoughts. Analyze the accuracy of the assumptions at the root of self-talk and negative self-talk. Replace these beliefs with more realistic and positive thoughts that allow you to grow and flourish.

Self-awareness and mindfulness Develop mindfulness by practicing mindful practices to increase self-awareness, and to be aware of your thoughts, and feelings without judgement. When you are in the present and observing your thoughts, you will be able to identify negativity in yourself as a fleeting thought and decide to not engage with these thoughts. Training in mindfulness can assist in keeping your focus towards the good things in your existence and in the present moment.

Honor Your Strengths: Highlight your achievements and strength. Write down your talents, qualities as well as achievements. Keep in mind these positive characteristics frequently, especially in times of self-talk that is negative. Recognize your strengths and apply them to boost confidence in yourself and build resilience.

Positive Self-Care: Choose self-care practices that nourish your body, mind and soul an important mainstay. Take time to engage in activities which bring joy and peace. It includes self-care practices like fitness, getting enough sleep and eating healthy food, taking time to be with nature and indulgence into hobbies that will make you feel happy.

Personal development and continuous learning Make sure you invest in your own individual growth and development. Explore opportunities to build new abilities, discover activities, and increase your understanding. Learning continuously boosts confidence in yourself and brings new ideas which can change your conversations.

GUIDED IMAGERY and VISUALIZATION Make use of guided imagery and visualization to produce pleasant mental images as well as experiences. Imagine yourself overcoming obstacles in your way, accomplishing your goals, as well as demonstrating a positive and confident mental attitude. Utilize these images regularly to boost self-esteem and inspire actions.

Here are some fascinating and practical ideas to cultivate an empowering and caring internal dialogue

Think of yourself as your person to be with, giving compassion, assistance, and compassion.

Replace self-criticism by self-confidence, saying to yourself, you're doing a great job.

Thoughts that are negative should be questioned by asking whether they are real or beneficial.

Be proud of even the smallest achievements and achievements throughout the journey.

Accept your imperfections and view your flaws as a an aspect of being truly human.

Take your time through difficult moments, and know that you are worthy of it.

Find people who can inspire and lift your spirits.

Make time every day to thank yourself for qualities that you admire about you.

Be yourself, and be happy just as you are. Be aware that you deserve satisfaction and happiness.

Don't compare yourself with others in the knowledge that everybody follows their own path.

Accept forgiveness for any mistakes you have made and realize that mistakes lead to improvement and development.

Build confidence in your capabilities and your potential by knowing you're equipped to achieve your goals.

Engage in activities that will keep you satisfied and allows you to be your authentic self.

Make achievable goals that reflect the values you hold dear, and be proud of your achievements in the process.

You should be credited and acknowledged for your effort made in your post.

Mindfulness lets you observe your thoughts and feelings without judgement which improves self-awareness.

Refrain from negative self-talk by using positive, empowering words to counter negative self-talk.

You can explore and share your feelings through healthy, productive ways.

Find answers instead of then waffling over problems, and you'll be able to make a decision.

Explore new possibilities and opportunities to grow and learn.

Spend time with yourself, and do exercises that improve and sustain your wellbeing.

The practice of deep breathing can aid you in achieving inner tranquility and ease stress.

Think about your strengths and abilities Be aware of the distinct qualities that distinguish you.

Inspire yourself by using positive words and affirmations or even messages.

Form a group of people who are able to understand and help your goals.

Make positive self-talk a part of your daily routine to help boost your self-esteem and confidence.

In difficult times, demonstrate empathy by showing compassion and comfort.

Be honest and open by embracing your being vulnerable as a virtue.

Make sure you are confident in your communication skills by communicating your thoughts and desires.

Your actions should align in line with your values while remaining true to you and your convictions.

Consider failure to be an opportunity to learn and grow to see it as the first step towards the next level of success.

Instead of seeking validation from outside or praise, you should focus in your personal growth.

Keep your mind stimulated with stimulating books, podcasts or TED Talks that expand your perspective.

Create visual reminders of your dreams and goals to help keep you focused and on track.

Let go of yourself and other people Let go of anger Find peace.

Take part in artistic actions that permit you to create and discover new passions.

In order to gain an understanding of your emotions and thoughts Make your time for reflection and journaling.

Be in touch with nature, and experience tranquility and peace through its natural beauty and tranquility.

Recognize your body for everything it allows you to achieve.

Find a fascination and enjoy lifelong learning development.

Establish appropriate boundaries and stress self-care in order to safeguard your wellbeing.

Share love and optimism by doing small acts of kindness for your fellow human beings and yourself.

Take on challenges with a positive attitude and see challenges as opportunities for personal development.

Find your passions and interests Then, take time to pursue them with passion.

It is possible to incorporate mindfulness into daily activities through noticing every moment, and taking joy in everyday things.

Imagine your goals and dreams like they've already been fulfilled, which will boost your confidence and motivation.

Get involved in regular physical exercise or exercise that boosts your mood and overall well-being.

You should surround yourself with friendly and positive individuals who encourage and inspire you.

Release yourself from self-criticism and accept yourself as a person, believing that you're deserving of compassion and love.

Be confident in your own abilities and in the power of your own inner voice to influence your daily life positively.

Be aware that creating a positive and inspiring inner conversation can be a lifetime endeavor. The patience, self-reflection as well as regular exercise are necessary. Through the journey, you must keep your self-love in check taking each step in the right direction, and appreciating every move and learning by overcoming challenges. When you develop your inner voice and you'll see a change in the way you view yourself and your world. It will result in increased self-love and confidence and a sense of empowerment.

Chapter 6: Strengthening Your Relationships Through Effective Communication

Communication is the foundation for satisfying and healthy relationships. It serves as a bridge between two people, fostering trust, respect, and intimacy. Communicating However, communication can be difficult. Communication that is truly listening and expressive is a matter of intention, ability and the ability to be listened. In this blog we'll look at how to bridge gaps by using effective communication. We will give valuable insights as well as practical methods to strengthen your interpersonal relationships. Learning to master the art of communication can help you build stronger connections and deal with issues without a fuss, whether it's in your relationship with family members, friends as well as friends and coworkers.

Listening Actively:

The act of listening actively is a crucial element of effective communication. It involves paying complete attentively to the speaker, without interfering or responding in a hurry. It is a sign of respect and validation the opinions of another person's opinions by completely listening. Make eye contact, smile to indicate understanding, and ask questions that clarify the situation for an active and attentive listening.

Communication that isn't non-verbal

Keep in mind that communication involves more than just words. Other clues can be just as significant. Pay attention to the way you look, your facial emotion, as well as your tone of speech. Your nonverbal communication needs to correspond to your spoken words, demonstrating the openness, understanding and sincerity.

Emotional Intelligence (EQ):

The ability to recognize emotions is crucial in effective communication. It is the ability to understand and manage the emotions of yourself as well as being able to recognize and empathizing with the feelings of other people. The ability to communicate with compassion and be able to respond to other their feelings in a caring and compassionate way if you develop emotional ability.

Needs and Desires Expression:

A healthy relationship requires the ability to communicate clearly and effectively the needs and wants of both parties. For you to express your emotions you should practice using "I" phrases rather than making accusations or blaming others. In expressing your needs make sure you are precise and offer instances to make sure your message gets through in a clear and understandable manner.

Dispute Resolution:

Unavoidable conflicts in relationships However, how you manage they can be a catalyst to strengthen or tear down the relationship. If there is a disagreement, approach the issue from a solution-focused perspective. Be focused on solving problems to find compromises and prepare to listen to the opposing point of perspective. Find a solution that is win-win through practicing compassion and empathy.

Conscious Communication:

Stay aware and present to your feelings, thoughts, and emotions to integrate awareness to your conversations. A mindful approach to communication allows you to make a response instead of reacting in an impulsive manner. Prior to responding you should take some time to contemplate and pick the words and actions you will use which are positive and aligned to your goal.

Empathy and Validation:

Empathy and validation are powerful ways to bridge gaps in understanding. Engage in genuine concern for perspectives and experiences of people around you. Accept and respect their opinions even when you don't necessarily agree. Be a sympathetic listener and provide a helping hand whenever they encounter difficulties.

Curiosity Development:

Begin conversations with a feeling of wonder, and a real desire to know. For a better connections, you should ask questions to encourage deeper discussion. The pursuit of curiosity creates an atmosphere where people feel valued as well as appreciated and encouraged to talk about their thoughts and experiences.

Communication that is sensitive to culture:

It is essential to understand the various cultural variations in the way you communicate and the way of life in today's multicultural world. Learn about and be respectful of the cultures of people around you, and adjust the way you communicate. In order to build diversity and create a the foundation for a safe space for discussion, you must embrace sensitivity to culture.

Active Reaction:

Feedback is essential for development and growth. You must be thorough, thoughtful and compassionate when you give criticism. Instead of attacking the individual focus on the behavior or circumstance. Be willing to listen to criticism and consider them as an opportunity to gain development of your own self and development.

Empathic listening practice Empathic listening goes beyond active listening. It involves putting yourself in the shoes of another person and fully understanding their perspective as well as responding with compassion and empathy. For accuracy, you must practice an empathetic listening style by trying to understand the emotion behind the words they speak, confirming the experiences they have shared, and then reflecting the information you receive.

Honesty and authenticity: In order to create good relationships integrity, honesty and sincerity are essential. You must be honest with yourself and other people by honestly sharing your feelings, thoughts and thoughts. In order to avoid being judged, try not to hide or denouncing your real self. Be yourself and be vulnerable. the right environment to have an open and honest conversation.

Limiting assumptions and judgments to a minimum. Incorrect assumptions and judgements could hinder the effectiveness of communications. Instead of thinking you know the meaning of someone's words or making a judgment about them, request clarification and seek out more details. Engage with people with openness, putting off your judgment until you understand the entire situation.

Building Patience and Understanding Effective communication demands understanding and patience. Don't jump to conclusions or interrupting others. Give others the freedom to speak their minds, and make sure you understand the meaning before responding. Show compassion and empathy even in the face of opposing opinions.

Instead of avoiding the possibility of confrontation, see it as the chance to develop and deeper connections. Consider disagreements as an opportunity to understand the other person and to find an understanding. When you are in disagreement, listen and seek out mutually beneficial solutions.

If you are faced with challenges or disputes, you must develop an active approach to problem solving. Instead of dwelling on the issue, focus on solving the issue. Work with other people to develop concepts and then work towards finding a solution. Keep in mind that establishing a common understanding and pushing ahead to achieve the goals of effective communications.

cultivating gratitude and positivity: Through conversations, develop positive and grateful interactions. Recognize others' presence and contribution. Honor their accomplishments and talents as you create a welcoming and inspiring work environment. Honor milestones and celebrate anniversaries with colleagues.

Establishing Boundaries: A healthy communication requires the setting and respect for the boundaries. Be clear about your boundaries to your coworkers and remain willing to accept the other. Boundaries give you a sense of protection by ensuring that each person's needs and requirements are being met.

Mindful Conflict Words Take note of phrases you employ during conflicts. Do not blame, critique, or launching personal attack. Instead, try making use of "I" expressions to describe what the issue is directly affecting your life. Keep cool, speak in a respectful manner, and employ the language that encourages cooperation and understanding.

Releasing Responsibility for Communication Effective communication involves a cooperative effort. Be accountable for your part in the process of communication. Be accountable of your behavior, words and actions and the way they impact others. Be clear, be attentive, and modify your behavior as needed.

Use humor and lightness to help: Mixing humor and lightness in conversations can alleviate tension and help create a positive setting. In order to lighten the mood and foster a sense of camaraderie and connection, employ a suitable form of humor. But keep the overall context in mind. Ensure that your joke is accepted by everyone in the event.

Polite Communication: Always be courteous when you communicate even in the most difficult of situations. Be gracious by remaining at peace, calm and well-organized. Beware of engaging in heated arguments or rushing to respond. Use words that encourage and help build bridges instead of words that tear them down.

Active Reflection: Consider your skills and behaviors in communication often. Be aware of the way your actions and words influence others as well as what you are able to do with your interactions. Take note of areas to improve and put in a concerted effort to develop and improve in your communication skills.

The ability to adapt and be flexible are the prerequisites to ensure effective communication. Prepare to alter your method of communication to meet the needs of

The ability to adapt and be flexible are the two main requirements to be able to communicate effectively. It is important to be able to adapt your approach to communication to accommodate the needs of different individuals, tastes as well as situations. Be aware that not all people communicate exactly the same way and then be open to changing the way you communicate to ensure understanding and communication.

Mindful Digital Communication the digital world of today communications are often conducted by means of screens. While communicating via online channels or technology, try to be mindful. Take note of the tone you use in your messages be careful with your choice of words, and limit confusion by ensuring clarity and context. Instead of becoming obstacles for effective communication, utilize digital tools to improve the connections.

Expression of Appreciation: Show gratitude for the efforts and contributions of other people. Be aware of their accomplishments and convey your gratitude to them for being in your daily life. Simple thank-you or a heartfelt message can help to build relationships and help create an environment of communication that is pleasant.

Active Collaboration: Effective communication requires collaboration. Find ways to collaborate and involve others in the decision-making process. Consider their contributions and create an inclusive atmosphere where every person's perspective and view is considered. Instill a sense belonging and shared responsibility within your relationships through active participation.

Refraining from Assumptions: They could lead to miscommunication and failures to communicate. Don't assume you know what they are saying or thinking, ask for clarification. Make sure you understand the perspective of their person prior to jumping into conclusion. The ability to ask questions and be curious could help you to gain more information and help avoid unnecessary arguments.

Timing with a sense of purpose The importance of timing is in effective communications. Take into consideration the most appropriate moment to begin important discussions. Take into consideration the person's attitude and level of accessibility. Choose a time when both parties are willing to having a meaningful conversation. Increase your odds for a successful and productive communications by ensuring you are aware of your timing.

Reflective listening involves paraphrasing and reviewing what the speaker spoken to gain the same understanding. Once the speaker is done speaking, consider re-visiting to them the things you've heard in order in order to confirm that you have understood the message they are trying to convey. This technique demonstrates your commitment to understanding while confirming the speaker's viewpoint.

Positive Feedback: Concentrate on being constructive instead of criticism when giving feedback. Offer specific details and suggest ways to improve. Instead of demotivating or dissuading your partner, frame your feedback to promote the growth of your colleague and encourage them to make progress. Feedback constructively aids in building trust as well as the growth of relations.

Understanding Nonverbal Cues: The nonverbal signals, like the facial expressions of a person's body could provide valuable details about someone's emotions and opinions. In conversations, pay attentively to these signals for a deeper comprehension of the content. The ability to react more efficiently and with greater empathy if you can detect non-verbal signals.

Active Conflict Resolution Conflict is a necessary part of any relationship. If there is a conflict, resolve these issues from a proactive solution-oriented perspective. Try to find ways to reach a common understanding and options that will benefit all parties. Conflict resolution involves attentively listening, clearly communicating your needs and desires as well as trying to find the possibility of compromise.

Genuineness in Expression A key element of authentic and authentic communication is authenticity. You must be honest and express your feelings, thoughts, and thoughts. If you want to please others, stay away from trying to conform or agree with them. Let yourself be vulnerable and create space for authentic, genuine dialog that builds connections.

Empathy can be defined as the capacity to understand and feel the emotions of someone else. Learn to develop empathy by placing yourself in the shoes of individual you are interacting with and trying to be able to see their perspective. The evidence of empathy can be seen by being aware of their feelings and experiences and responding with compassion.

Setting Communication Objectives:

Set communication goals for you and your contacts. Find areas that need improvement including active listening, and dispute resolution.

Set Communication Goals: Create your communication goals as well as your contacts. Look for areas to improve like being active in listening, conflict resolution and successfully communicating emotions. Reduce these goals into steps that you can manage and be consistent in achieving them. Set goals for communication helps you track your progress, and to continue to develop as a communicator.

Fostering Open-Mindedness: Engage in communication with an open-minded mind as well as an ability to accept different perspectives. Do not become rigid or enslaved to your personal convictions. Learn from people around you and increase your perspectives. Fostering an open mind creates a welcoming atmosphere and encourages different perspectives.

Building trust: Solid relations are built on trust. Make sure you establish trust by engaging in an honest and open conversation. Make sure you keep your word, stay quiet, and stay constant in your actions and actions. It creates a comfortable atmosphere for honest and open conversations, and allows relationships to grow.

Respecting Differences: Each person is unique in their perspectives, beliefs and beliefs. When you communicate, bear these differences at the forefront. Instead of making opinions or assumptions basing your decisions on different opinions, try to accept and appreciate diverse points of view. Respectful communication fosters understanding and builds connections.

The power of communication can enable both yourself and other people. With positive and encouraging language can help you inspire and lift those in your circle. Honor their talents accomplishments, achievements, and distinct traits. If you help others to be successful by empowering them, you create a positive environment which encourages growth and encouragement and support.

The process of building Rapport: Rapport is the relationship and the understanding that is created between two people. Create rapport with real relaxation and active participation in discussions. Discover common ground, make questions that are open to discussion, and demonstrate curiosity about the experiences and lives of others. The building of rapport is a source of trust, which allows better communications.

The Mindful Body Language body language may transmit the amount of information you convey through your words, if not even more. Take note of your body language while speaking. Keep a relaxed and open position, maintain eye contact and use gentle gestures. Keeping your body aware enhances the clarity and effectiveness of your communications.

In even the best of conversation, miscommunications could happen. When confusions arise, you must be patient and quick to resolve them. Be clear on your goals, get clarification from the person you disagree with as well as keep an open mind to reaching a compromise. Dissolving disputes helps keep from future conflicts and build relations.

Growing gratitude: In your communications, show your gratitude and acknowledgement. Consider the contribution and help of other people. Be grateful and give them the specific ways in which your efforts have helped you.

The act of gratitude creates a positive atmosphere for communication and strengthens relationships with others.

Utilizing "I" phrases: Instead instead of blaming others or making accusations, make use of "I" phrases to communicate your feelings or thoughts. "I" statements take ownership of the feelings and experience you have that promote understanding and lessens the need to defend. So, for instance Instead of declaring "You Always ...""", you can say "I am feeling ..."

The process of active conflict prevention is more than just settling disputes but also the prevention of conflicts from occurring. Be open in your communication be quick to resolve issues and develop patience and compassion to try to prevent conflict. Improve your interpersonal relationship by dealing with issues prior to them escalating.

Be mindful of your digital Etiquette A well-informed digital manner of conduct is essential in this modern age. Make sure you are aware of your web presence and the way your words could be misinterpreted. Be respectful of your language, avoid from inflicting insults and observe the rules of other people. Make use of digital technology to help encourage respect and positive interaction.

Develop Flexibility: Communication is a continuous process which demands adaptability. Adjust your style of communication to the various situations and individuals. You should be able to adapt to different style of communication and alter your style as required. Flexibility helps to ensure more efficient and effective processes.

The development of flexibility in communication is a continuous process which demands adaptability. Adjust your style of communication to the various situations and individuals. Accept a variety of ways of communicating and adjust your method as necessary. Flexibility allows for better communications and demonstrates your ability to work with people on a different level.

Self-Reflection: Consider your communication style and actions often. Examine how you influence the conversations you have with others and how they affect your interactions. Take note of whether you exhibit the tendency to dominate discussions in a noisy manner, disrupt others' conversations and have a problem with actively listening. Self-reflection can help you pinpoint points for improvement, and it also helps increase the self-awareness of the person who communicates.

Chapter 7: Becoming The Hero Of Your Journey

The journey of life is filled with ups and downs as well as triumphs, struggles, and challenges. Every person is a different tale to tell and it's in that story that we hold the power to decide our destiny. It is possible to improve our lives by creating a story which inspires and motivates the people around us through embracing our potential and becoming the protagonist of our story. In this article we'll look at the best way to tell your own empowered narrative, explore your own capabilities, and then become the hero of your story.

Accepting your Self-Awareness is the initial step towards creating your own empowered narrative. Spend the time to discover more about yourself, your beliefs along with your strengths as well as the flaws. Examine your life's events in detail and the way they have shaped your life. The ability to be aware helps you identify the areas that need improvement, build upon your talents and take conscious choices that reflect the person you are.

Setting Goals: Choose your goals and what you'd like to be. Make specific goals to your journey, be it the development of your professional career, personal improvement and establishing relationships. Your goals function as a compass that guides your decisions and actions and guiding you along your path to success.

The importance of taking responsibility: Being accountable for your actions gives you the strength. Accept that you have the power to change your life and make choices in line with your ideals. Recognize that you're not an unfortunate victim and instead, you are the creator of your own destiny.

Take Charge of Your Narrative You are in control of the story you tell. Be aware of your capacity to interpret your past experience and write the narrative in ways that allow you to be more effective. Make mistakes as an opportunity for transformation and growth.

Instead of dwelling on the apparent difficulties or setbacks, opt to concentrate on learnings learned and the skills gained.

Finding Limiting Beliefs: Review and challenge your negative beliefs. The past, your social upbringing and self-doubt can affect these beliefs. Change negative self-talk into affirmations that build you up. Build a positive mindset which is open to new possibilities and trusts in your ability to conquer obstacles.

Growing Resilience: Resilience can be described as the capacity to overcome hardship. Build resilience through learning methods of coping, asking for assistance when needed as well as practicing self-care. Take challenges as opportunities to growth, and view obstacles as temporary roadblocks that can be overcome to achieve the goal.

Action and goals Make clear, quantifiable and achievable objectives that align with your empowering tale. Separate them into manageable parts and create a strategy for your journey. When you progress and change as you grow, make sure to review and alter your objectives regularly.

Believing in Courage: It takes courage to be the protagonist of your journey. Be bold and take a step beyond your familiar zone. Be open to uncertainty and believe in the potential of your abilities. Be brave enough to follow your interests, show the person you are, and take decisions that are reflective of your authentic self.

Establishing a Strong Network Begin by forming a network of people who are committed to you and the path you're on. Find mentors, friends or groups that will inspire and encourage you. Talk about your hopes and struggles with them. Let their support and encouragement boost your development.

Being gentle with yourself: Be kind and compassionate to yourself. Be proud of your achievements regardless of how small or insignificant, and then forgive yourself of the slightest mistakes. You should treat yourself with the same kindness and compassion the way you would treat an intimate family member.

Be open to change: Consider it as a normal element of the journey. Be aware that in order to progress one must step outside the comfort zones, and accept different experiences. Be open to change as a way to explore yourself and develop your personal skills.

Adopting Empathy: Gain compassion for others and yourself. Try to understand the thoughts and emotions of the people in your life. Genuine listening and compassion must be cultivated. When you practice empathy, it could strengthen your connections and build a more supportive and understanding work environment.

Integrity: Always be in your own truth and beliefs and values. Being authentic involves being able to share your thoughts, emotions as well as desires being true to your personal style and your authentic self be seen.

Accepting the Growth mindset Adopting a Growth mindset where you see challenges as opportunities to learn and grow. Believe that your skills and abilities can be improved through determination and hard work. A growth mindset allows you to take on the challenges you face with a willingness to grow.

Learning to cultivate gratitude: Develop a habit of gratitude by acknowledging and appreciating things that are good within your own life. Every day, take time to think about your gratitude for what you have regardless of whether it's your loved ones' support as well as your achievements or even your own natural beauty. Being grateful draws your focus towards the beauty that surrounds you and encourages positive attitude.

Becoming Knowledge-driven: Assume the pursuit of knowledge and growth throughout your life. Find new information as well as experiences in line with your interests and goals. Take part in workshops, read books as well as take classes as well as participate in other activities which broaden your perspective and allow you to grow.

Building Resilience through the development of a positive mind and having the capacity to face challenges. Take setbacks as merely temporary challenges that can be used to gain knowledge. Have a positive outlook and trust in your ability to conquer difficulties.

Making self-care an integral part of your journey. Be mindful of your mental, physical and emotional well-being. Meditation, exercise, in the outdoors, or engaging in hobbies you are passionate about are all actions which will nourish and rejuvenate your energy.

Accepting Accountability: Be accountable for your choices and actions. Take responsibility for the mistakes you made and then learn from your mistakes. Create goals that are big for you and set out to meet these goals. If you are willing to take responsibility and committing to yourself, you grant yourself the opportunity to charge of the process.

Learning to Adapt: Since things are constantly evolving, developing adaptability helps you to navigate the turns and twists of your path. Learn to accept change and be able to adapt to changing conditions. Being flexible gives you the chance to take risks and create new strategies.

Recognizing Reflection: Take time for reflection and self-reflection. Review your progress frequently and review your options change your course whenever necessary. Retrospective helps you remain on the right track with your own story, and to take informed decision-making.

Milestones:

Be proud of your achievements on your journey, regardless of what they might seem. Be proud of your achievements and be proud of the actions you've taken. Recognizing your accomplishments boosts confidence and boosts motivation of your abilities.

Asking for Help: Understand that seeking help can be a sign of confidence and not insecurity. If you need help, ask assistance from friends, mentors or even professionals. Be surrounded by people who are able to inspire you and inspire you to succeed.

Be patient: Remember that personal transformation and growth require some time. Take your time and trust that you can accomplish it. Take care of yourself and allow yourself to improve, develop and change.

Establishing healthy limits: Make healthy boundaries that protect your wellbeing and meet the needs of your body. Be clear about your boundaries and without hesitation. Boundaries allow you to create an enlightened and tranquil travel experience.

Engaging in Self-Reflection: Rethink your journey and the experiences you've gained regularly. It's a good idea to take a moment to reflect about the progress you've made.

Mindfulness Training: Learn to remain present and involved in your journey. Be aware of your feelings, thoughts, and feelings. The practice of mindfulness allows you to take more deliberate decisions and to respond to the situation faster.

Being vulnerable to yourself Accepting Yourself to Be Vulnerable: Let yourself allow yourself to be vulnerable as well as open experiences that are new. Be willing to feel the pain caused by stepping out of your familiar zone. There are opportunities to grow as well as stronger bonds with other people through accepting your the vulnerability.

Learning to forgive: Learn how to shed bitterness and resentments. Release past wounds and let go of the emotional burden that's keeping you from moving forward. Moving forward, you can have a more peace of mind and a renewed peace of mind by practicing forgiveness.

Being Flexible: Be flexible to the possibility of changing your goals and your expectations. Prepare yourself for deviations and unanticipated opportunities on the road. Flexibility allows you to adapt to and take advantage of unpredictable situations.

Instilling Optimism: Develop optimism that is focused on positive outcomes. Be confident in your ability to conquer obstacles and create your ideal life. A positive outlook helps you remain positive even in the face of hardship.

Being Real: Be honest and original in your approach. Explore ways of expressing yourself through writing, painting music or other art form that appeals to your. Self-expression allows you express your individual voice with the world.

Maintaining curiosity: Have your mind open and have a desire to learn. Be open to thoughts, ideas and new experience. The pursuit of knowledge keeps your mind active and helps you progress.

Relaxing and Reflecting: Take some time to contemplate and reflect. Consider your values, convictions and dreams frequently. Consider your past memories and learnt from your experiences. Reflection increases your self-awareness, and helps you plan your actions.

Empathy is developed by trying to connect to people on a deeper levels. Try to put yourself in their shoes and engage in active listening. Empathy enhances relationships and increases your sense of empathy.

Engaging in Genuine Connections: Create long-lasting relationships based on trust, honesty and mutual trust. Connect with those who can inspire and motivate you. Make meaningful connections that feed your soul and assist you in continuing to develop.

Develop a growth mindset Develop a mindset of growth that believes in your capacity to improve change, grow, and develop. Take setbacks as a chance to improvement, while failing can be a way to achievement. A growth mindset lets you grow.

Being Self-Compassionate: Be kind to yourself, compassionate, and understanding towards yourself. Make sure you take care of yourself as well as your health. Self-compassion is a foundation to personal growth and resilience.

To cultivate authenticity, one must be true to oneself, and respecting the values, interests aspirations, and values. Let your uniqueness shine through and let your real personality be seen. Being authentic allows you to be true to who you are.

Believing in Balance: Find harmony in every aspect of your life. This includes your relationships, work as well as self-care and personal growth. You can achieve balance by prioritizing the health of your body, setting limits and making the time to do what's truly significant for you.

Making an effort to do self-reflection and reflection frequently. Writing, meditation and other practices which help you connect to your own inner self is recommended. The process of self-reflection helps you understand yourself better and can lead to improvement.

Accepting Accountability: You must take responsibility of your choices, actions as well as the results. Keep yourself accountable for your progress and the outcome you get. Be accountable for your actions and your impact in your life.

Self-Belief: Be confident in your abilities and yourself. Build a solid sense of self-confidence that motivates you even in the face of difficulties or doubts. Be confident in yourself and strength.

Accepting gratitude: Show appreciation for the blessings in your life and opportunities. Enjoy small moments, the company of your loved ones, as well as the lessons you have learned from the turbulence. By practicing gratitude, you can direct your focus towards the abundance that surrounds you.

Develop Adaptability: Enhance the ability of your brain to adjust and change to the changing environment. Take the uncertainties as a possibility to learn and grow. Being flexible lets you manage life's changes by perseverance and grace.

Adopting authenticity: Be yourself as you really are, and release your need to conform to expectations set by other people. Stay true to yourself in your thinking, behavior as well as your relationships. Believing in authenticity can help you have authentic connections and brings happiness.

Mind-Body connection: Be aware of the complex connection that is present between your body and your mind. Maintain your physical well-being by working out as well as eating a balanced diet and taking enough time off. Engage in activities like yoga or meditation that help strengthen your mind-body connection.

Discovering Yourself: Research to learn more about yourself. Take part in activities that stimulate your curiosity and give you satisfaction. Begin to explore your inner self in the process of learning more about who you are and the opportunities.

Setting Healthy Boundaries: Set safe boundaries that safeguard your time, energy and overall well-being. In the event of a need, be able to say no, and prioritize your requirements. The boundaries foster a sense self-esteem and promote healthy relationships.

In the end, be grateful for the entirety of your journey, which includes all the lows and highs. Accept that the challenges you experience and the learnings learned will contribute to an increase in your self-esteem and confidence. Take the opportunity to become the main character in your own tale.

Chapter 8: Dbt And Its Core Principles

The mind is a huge complex of emotional complexities and mental health can hover at the edge of an immense gap. The mind's realm that has been explored by scholars as diverse as Shakespeare, Plato, Archimedes, Leonardo da Vinci, and William James, has perpetually amazed us all, challenging the perception of the mind, reality and what life is all about. It's no surprise because we have no direct insight into its inner workings. Therefore our perception of ourselves and other people is mostly an outcome of our own perceptions and the interpretations we make.

Even with the best intentions, the vast and shady world known as the mind could be a major influence on the essential elements of our lives despite being aware. If a person's feelings or behaviour is in conflict with their values, it can create a situation that is "wheels within wheels" as they try to control and manage the subsequent chaos. When these issues arise those who are affected often suffer from emotional disorders like anxiety, depression, or addiction. In the absence of assistance from a professional, strategies for coping like substance abuse excessive exercise, perfectionism and self-mutilation can appear as brief getaways.

DBT is a method of restoring an orderly and emotional exhausting landscape by correcting maladaptive ways of thinking and behaviour. It acknowledges that feelings aren't a separate thing from the ability to think. In fact, thoughts and emotions are inextricably linked and must be treated in order to obtain maximum therapeutic benefits over the long term.

DBT is focused on helping people "ride the waves" of emotion more effectively and with less anxiety. The person who's proficient with the techniques provided by DBT is less likely be impulsive and will be more likely to respond with a rational and thoughtful approach to events they confront. However, there's more to the practice than just talk therapy.

UNDERSTANDING DIALECTICS: THE BALANCE OF OPPOSITES

The idea that there is a "balance of opposites" is an integral part of two of the three basic theories of dialectics.

Everything is interconnected.

Opposites may be combined into a better representation of the real.

The pace of change is always changing and is inevitable.

To expand on these ideas It is crucial to understand that elements in conflict engage with each other in a dynamic, reciprocal interaction. To better understand the significance of this notion, we'll look at the old Chinese philosophy of yin and Yang. This concept demonstrates that opposites do not just interdependent but that their peaceful interdependence is vital for the success of every systems.

Think about the many natural systems that we live in, displaying you can see the distinct energies of Yang (representing femininity, darkness quietness, calmness contemplation, passivity and quiet) and the yang (embodying the masculine, the light activation, heat and energy) are seamlessly integrated to create the whole of. In this dance of opposite forces that the idea of dialectics has its origins that depict a universe where conflict is the fuel that sustains the whole order and sustains the existence of dialectics.

In this delicate system each player has a the greatest importance; each component, regardless what it is and function, plays a pivotal role. If one component fails or cease to function, the delicate balance can be disrupted, resulting in a ripple that could result in the collapse of the whole system. A dialectical view of the world can prompt us to take on a more sophisticated lens with which to look at the world. It also helps to develop awareness of the crucial function of balance in the tug and pull of forces that are at odds.

This duality is also present in the human psyche. There are positive and negative elements that need to be balanced as do the justice scales. This is why the human brain is prone to react in extreme circumstances that involve emotional turmoil by forming abnormal, often maladaptive behaviors which could result in abnormal mental states.

In this way, the idea of "balancing opposites" gains practical importance in everyday life. It can be vital to keeping mental sanity. How do you find this equilibrium?

AVOID EXTREME VIEWPOINTS AND "ALL OR NOTHING" REASONING

The dangerous fallacy in "all-or-nothing" thinking can significantly alter our understanding regarding the reality. It can lead us to classify things in stark contrast like white or black, the right or wrong way, and ignores the inherent complexity and subtleties. But, the reality of life doesn't fit well into binary categorizations. It is instead awash with shades of grey in which things may not always be so clear as they initially appear.

When faced with complex scenarios there are times when we will come across opposing views and none of them can give the whole truth. Thus, gaining a deeper awareness of the complicated dialectic will allow individuals to deal with such scenarios in a more flexible and nuanced manner that can help us develop a better and more realistic view of the world we live in.

In the case of two parents, they could disagree over the best timing to collect their kids from school, or the appropriate way to let them access smartphones. Parents aren't able agree on a solution so endless discussions at the table result. That's where mindfulness could help.

Mindfulness refers to living in the moment, without judgment of the event or according to according to the Oxford English Dictionary makes clear, "It is the quality or state of being conscious or aware of something." The practice draws on the long-standing Buddhist practice of mindfulness and is now being used in the modern world of secular as well as therapeutic practices to enhance well-being, ease stress and increase self-awareness.

The ability to be mindful is something which we can improve with time that will help us develop an more balanced way of thinking, instead of becoming stuck in rigid beliefs that hinder healthy dialog. In the above situation, parents could be able to see that their partners' opinions have merit, and discover a commonality that pleases each other.

If you're mindful, do not make use of the terms "always" or "never" in analyzing an issue in a way that they overemphasize absolutes and reject the possibility of different perspectives. Instead, consider every aspect of the situation in a neutral way to gain clarity and unbiasedness.

AVOID EXPRESSING BELIEFS OR OPINIONS THAT ARE BASED ON CONFLICTING CLAUSES

Did you ever say, "I've been working hard to get promoted, but I don't think it's going to happen," or "I'm trying to lose weight, but I can't seem to achieve it?" You may have been making these claims for many years, but you're not aware of the truth behind it. What happens in these circumstances: You contradict your original statement with the reverse which creates a room for disappointment and ultimately feelings of regret, shame as well as guilt and stress.

Take it as follows Think about it this way: If you declare to be doing your best but don't have high expectations then you're most likely to receive exactly what you want because your brain anticipates the outcomes. If you show optimism and confidence the words you speak will serve as a prediction for positive outcomes. Thus, change those "but's" for "and's." It is possible to say "I've been working hard for this promotion, and I believe it will happen."

EMBRACE PHYSICAL BALANCE

This is an exercise that I personally recommend and endorse as a routine practice. It was a regular element of my daily routine a few some time ago, when I sought out a reliable way to reduce anxiety and stress. The effect was significant. It's a simple exercise and involves sustaining stability while sitting or standing.

Start by standing up tall, with your weight evenly distributed across both feet. Or when sitting, make sure that you're in a straight chair and your weight is evenly distributed over both hips. Take note of the feel of your feet being on the floor or your thighs pressed against the chairs.

After inhaling deeply then lean slightly forward, exhale, then slowly back to your normal posture. Do the same exercise again, however this time, lower your body when you inhale, prior to exhaling and readjusting your body back to the original upright body posture. While you perform the exercises, be sure there is a balanced amount of weight distributed on each side of your leg.

The goal of this workout isn't only the physical aspect, but an evocative insistence on the necessity to maintain balance in our thinking as well as our emotional life. It's an easy, yet effective practice that will help create a sense of groundedness and stability in daily day life.

HISTORY AND PHILOSOPHY OF DBT

In order to fully grasp the scope and potential of DBT the concept, you must explore its origins and the philosophies that guide it. The concept was developed by Dr. Marsha M. Linehan in the latter part of the 1970s. DBT was born from the need to meet the unique needs of people who suffer from borderline personality disorder (BPD).

It was Dr. Linehan, cognizant of the limitations of traditional treatment methods like cognitive behavior therapy (CBT) and mindfulness meditation, as well as Eastern philosophical theories, realized the limitations of these methods in addressing the subtleties of BPD. So, she set out to come up with a fresh method that would be able to capture the complexity of human emotion and relationship and lay the foundation to develop DBT.

The Dr. Linehan had first-hand experience of mental disease. When she was a teenager she experienced profound feelings of emptyness and was prone to self-destructive behaviors as well as suicidal ideas. Her diagnosis was schizophrenia in the Institute of Living in Hartford, CT, where she was admitted in the year 1961. The seriousness of her illness caused her to be one of the toughest patients at the institution. In her stay of two years, she was subjected restriction, excessive medication as well as isolated confinement.

"Dr. Linehan recalls experiencing a memory loss following the treatment of electroconvulsive treatment (ECT). Then, she was referred to Cook County Insane Asylum, that, according to her described as an "Kafkaesque nightmare." However her vivid account did not contain any hint of disdain or negative feelings She expressed her immense appreciation for her caregivers who helped her open up to new ways of approaching the process of healing.

Dr. Linehan's experience of suffering and pain led her to assist other patients who suffer from the same issues "come out of hell." Her strategy was to balance behaviourism (CBT) with humanism as well as using a non-discriminatory approach that established a strong foundation for dialectics. Instead of holding meetings which could make people feel defensive as everyone pointed towards them as the culprit the doctor. Linehan offered a supportive environment that encouraged change, but also stressed self-reflection as well as validation.

This method led to DBT that was eventually popularly known as Zen behavioral therapy thanks to the Dr. Marsha's Zen training. This was the first method that incorporated mindfulness. And the best part was that it was not only beneficial to those suffering from serious mental illness or who suffer from BPD.

The concept of dialectics as a way of understanding and reconciling contradicting ideas is rooted in the past into the renown Greek philosophers, such as Socrates or Plato. In the past the dialectical approach was based on logic-based dialogues to reconcile two opposing concepts. Though dialectics is an area that is rooted in logic, the dialectical philosophy that is at the core of DBT recognizes the personal realities which might not be confined to the strictures of logic, yet are relevant within the individual's context.

DBT uses the principles of dialectical philosophy to serve as an instrument to achieve the right balance and clarity when treating, encouraging therapeutic relationships, as well as promoting general well-being. This is clearly demonstrated by its basic dichotomy between the acceptance of change and change the concept that was pioneered by Dr. Linehan. Dialectical thinking is practical flexible, adaptable, and useful even in the most difficult conditions.

It is not uncommon for therapists and counselors to sympathize with their clients, they some behaviors dangerous enough to not be tolerated. When this happens an uncompromising, clear position is taken, demonstrating the balance of validation and the necessity for change. This is a sign of DBT's dedication to encouraging healthier behavior and also acknowledges the individual's emotions and experiences.

CORE PRINCIPLES OF DBT

Dialectical behavioral therapy is founded on the four core principles of mindfulness and distress tolerance, as well as emotion control, and interpersonal efficiency.

MINDFULNESS

Being mindful means being fully engaged with the present, taking note of every aspect of your environment -- taking in the gentle rhythms of your life, savoring the warmth of the sun's rays upon your skin, and savoring the awe-inspiring quality of one second, and not having the slightest hint of judgement. In the context of DBT this search for peace amid the chaos helps in getting through the maze of one's mind with a sense of clarity and poise.

In fostering a more acute awareness of your emotions, thoughts and body sensations you can make room for conscious choices to support the healing process and development. As a therapist I counsel clients to cultivate mindfulness by taking part in meditation, doing breathing exercises, and by learning to be aware of and articulate their feelings without becoming emotionally involved in the events. The approach helps them react to events with more understanding of themselves and a sense of emotional balance.

DISTRESS TOLERANCE

Just like a raging sea, life's storms can suddenly unleash powerful waves, which could threaten to shake our stability, and plunge our souls in despair. When we are in a difficult time the ability to tolerate distress is an anchor solid that holds us grounded, and prevents our being carried into the sea by the waves. In times of crisis it's normal to experience a variety of negative emotions, including anxiety, pain, and fear. In the absence of a connection to your own inner strength and resilience, you may react with impulsiveness and have counterproductive results.

Like the Dr. Linehan suggests, distress tolerance is a key factor in quickly restoring balance you are confronted by new stresses to prevent you from succumbing to the enticing but destructive way of reacting too much. Take, for example, encountering a person who is constantly complaining over their boss or job which pushes your limits of patience. The initial reaction could be anger, which could turn to a fight that increases the gap.

If you're grounded in calm and peace You have the ability to make this difficult situation an possibility. It is possible to constructively tackle the problem at hand by acknowledging the concerns of your friends and feelings, confirming their emotions, and offering alternatives.

EMOTIONAL REGULATION

Think of our lives as an orchestral concert that sees emotions grow and decrease and create the ever-changing melody and rhythm of our lives. Every emotion is a distinct instrument that contributes its own music to the whole. However, what happens if the music becomes chaotic and the notes get jumbled and create an unsettling clatter, instead of an exquisite music?

When this happens, the emotional regulation serves as the expert conductor of the orchestra. It helps to calm chaos, as well as aligns the individual notes into harmonious melodies and shrewdly steers us through our emotional score's inevitable crescendos as well as diminuendos.

The goal of emotional regulation isn't to silence those instruments that make you tense or improving the sound of pleasant music but rather, it's about recognizing each emotion and note and then integrating them into an enlightened and balanced composition. It requires us to acknowledge our feelings, and not as unwelcome disturbances, however as integral elements of the human experience.

DBT offers various effective methods developed to calm the turbulent emotional storms that arise and allow us to find harmony and peace amid the turbulent waters of our emotions. These techniques help us control emotions without suppressing their intensity, and encourage our bodies to be more responsive instead of reacting to emotional states.

Learn to recognize and recognize our emotions and their fluctuating nature and the impact they have on our thinking and actions. We are taught to describe our experiences precisely, learn how to modify our emotions so that they align with our goals and values in addition to how to live an emotionally more balanced life.

By observing the principles of DBT We learn not only how to navigate our emotions, but also recognize its complexity and depth. It is the essence that emotional regulation turns us from just spectators to our emotions into expert conductors that can harmonize the stunning, but complex symphony in our personal lives.

INTERPERSONAL EFFECTIVENESS

Healthy, fulfilling relationships are an essential part of the life as humans. According to the words of 17th century English writer John Donne, "No man is an island." Human beings, as social beings are inherently connected with other people. But navigating through the maze of human relationships isn't always easy. It's possible to stumble upon conflict and unwelcome invaders in our privacy or struggle with how to express our true self and being respectful.

Understanding these difficulties, DBT steps in with the essential ability to improve interpersonal communication. This concept goes far beyond the resolution of conflict or enhancement of communication. It focuses on encouraging understanding, increasing assertiveness, setting healthy boundaries and fostering compassion. The aim isn't just to "deal" with other people rather to strengthen the relationships we have with them and fill the relationships with genuine connections and respect for each other.

DBT gives us techniques to enhance our effectiveness in interpersonal relationships.

We are able to communicate our feelings and needs in a clear manner and respectfully. It also helps to create an atmosphere that encourages honesty and transparency in communications. Learn to find an equilibrium between respecting your personal boundaries while taking care of the boundaries of others in order to ensure that our interactions are beneficial to our wellbeing rather than hindering the quality of our lives.

Furthermore, interpersonal efficiency is extended to the resolution of conflicts. DBT offers practical methods for managing conflicts with respect and respect, opening the way to the resolution of conflicts instead of increasing. DBT encourages us all to choose the power of assertiveness and not be a victim to passiveness or aggression which allows us to assert the rights we have while also respecting the rights of other people.

The most important thing is that DBT emphasizes the importance of empathy when it comes to interpersonal effectiveness.

Knowing and sharing the experiences of other people helps us connect with others on a more of a personal level, creating better, more enjoyable connections. Through practicing empathy, we are able to transform our relationships as mere exchanges and occasions for mutual growth and connections.

The essence of interpersonal effectiveness is that capabilities transform the intricate interaction of humans into an elegant dance that will result in deeper healthy connections. Through DBT you can go from being a mere part of our community to flourishing within it, enhancing our relationships and the people that we share them with.

HOW DO THESE PRINCIPLES INTERACT AND SUPPORT EACH OTHER?

The great thing about DBT is the fact that each of its four components strengthens and complements the other. Take mindfulness as an example, which helps that you are conscious of your body and your thoughts. Mindfulness in this manner allows you to take a more "black-and-white" position, which helps regulate your emotions. It makes you less reactive and more adaptable and able to attain a state of calm.

Imagine that your last relationship ended due to your partner cheating on you. Recently, you've discovered someone who is a potential love-interest. One morning, your lover goes out for a girl or a guys' night out but doesn't reply to messages or phone calls and you are left with the horrible emotions of feeling betrayed. Are you quick to make a decision and go with your "no-contact" route, or just wait for them to get into contact to discuss the issue?

When you're someone who practice DBT and is a DBT practitioner, your actions will follow the guidelines you've chosen to adhere to. The practice of mindfulness creates a space which blocks out the past - - those hurts, disappointments or traumas which are not connected to the moment. When you are mindful, you can avoid the path of negative thinking that causes unnecessary emotional turmoil. You'll be able to remain in a calm, rational state.

The ability to tolerate stress is beneficial because it helps take the pain out of negativity. The ability to regulate your emotions can help you to gain insight into your life and make better decisions. Consider a moment to consider what is causing the agitated emotions and thoughts are gnawing at your mental peace and how to deal with this. Perhaps you'll need to go on a long stroll or watch the heartwarming show to get back to a state of equilibrium.

If you do finally meet your spouse, the interpersonal skills helps you to express your feelings and thoughts with the sensitivity and compassion you deserve. This way, you will stay clear of the traps of "sour grapes" and "he-said-she-said" tales and get to what is at the heart of it. It is possible to begin the discussion with the words, "Honey, I'm glad you enjoyed your ladies' evening out. I'm happy you got a time to unwind and recharge. It was however a little worrying that you did not answer my messages. I figured you may be experiencing some issues or perhaps drinking too much. Are you willing to share with me about what transpired?"

This method puts the ball on the court of your friend and enables your partner to take action. The other person could then say that they turned off their cell phone mode, and lost their track of the time. When they realize your concerns you'll want them to take steps to alleviate your anxiety, which could include reevaluating their actions. The situation wouldn't likely have occurred in the event that you'd behaved improperly.

The DBT principles offer a guideline that will help you develop the maturation you require to reach the true growth and healing.

DBT VS. CBT: HOW DO THEY DIFFER?

Dialectical Behavior Therapy (DBT) as well as Cognitive Behavior Therapy (CBT) are two powerful, scientifically-based strategies used to tackle different psychological problems. Both have a common foundation, but have distinct concepts and methods. These differences could make an important difference in the way they tackle certain ailments and what patients may gain the greatest benefits from each method.

The fundamental principle behind it is that CBT is focused on the process of cognitive restructuring. The focus of this method is on finding and changing the negative beliefs and thoughts that cause bad emotions and behavior. This technique allows people to question and modify their thoughts by providing the ability to control their emotions as well as their actions.

DBT On contrary, rests upon the dialectics principle that is, the reconciliation and balance of two opposing forces, specifically changes and acceptance. It recognizes the tension that exists between the need for individual change as well as the desire to accept oneself. The dual view allows for an individualized approach to treating and personal growth, and self-esteem while promoting self-confidence.

Although CBT therapists are likely to be more focused on challenging the patient's cognitive limitations, DBT therapists might adopt an approach that is more centered around validation especially with those who are suffering from severe issues with their emotional regulation. They aid patients in understanding the truth in their thinking and feelings, even if they appear to be in opposition to logic. The goal is to create an alliance of trust between the therapeutic team and decrease resistance towards treatments.

This is why DBT can be extremely helpful for those who do not be aware of their mental health problems or suffer from conditions that are characterized by intense emotional reactions like Borderline Personality Disorder and certain anxiety conditions. They may find

DBT's positive aspects DBT especially resonant and beneficial.

In the same way, the focus DBT puts on emotional and distress control can provide vital ways to cope for those struggling with addiction problems. These particular individuals can have issues with engagement when conventional CBT strategies are utilized because of how addiction manifests as well as the impact it has on cognition and emotional well-being. Through addressing these concerns specifically, DBT offers a more targeted and possibly effective treatment.

One of the unique advantages of DBT is the integration of mindfulness techniques and acceptance methods that are derived from Buddhist meditation practice. They promote self-compassion and allow patients to be aware of the thoughts and emotions they experience without judgment by bringing them into the actual moment. Incorporating mindfulness techniques enhances the tools for therapeutic use, giving a deeper therapy approach that combines mindfulness techniques and practices that emphasize self-awareness as well as acceptance.

To summarize, even though DBT and CBT have a common root and common objective of easing emotional distress, their differing theories and methods offer distinct methods of healing. Recognizing these distinctions will help the practitioners tailor their therapy method to the specific demands of each patient and help the patient better understand their own treatment process.

Chapter 9: Common Sense

The world we live in is quite hectic with a myriad of distractions, a constant stream is vying for our attention as well as a myriad of stresses are lurking in every direction. Finding peace of mind and tranquility is more difficult than it has ever been. Much like a twitching pendulum that is our mind, it oscillates between our past struggles and triumphs and our future goals which leaves little time to be present. If not controlled, this continuous state of "busyness" can alienate us from our environment and ourselves which can lead to a variety of mental, physical and psychological health issues.

The practice of mindfulness, which is the deliberate cultivation of awareness, provides an oasis of calm in the uncertain sea. It is rooted in the ancient tradition of contemplative meditation and gaining significant research-based validation, mindfulness allows people to live fully in the time. Through embracing every moment in a non-judgmental, open awareness, we will cultivate a higher level of awareness which promotes the process of self-discovery, inner peace and general well-being.

What do you expect of this section? This chapter is going to dive right into the core of mindfulness, shining some light on its fundamental principles and the profound impact it has on our emotional, psychological physical, and mental states. The course will also examine the various tried-and-true practices that are the basis of mindfulness and demonstrate practical strategies to integrate them seamlessly in everyday life.

You can expect to gain a deeper knowledge of how this significant method can result in an improved level of consciousness, enhanced emotional control, better relations with others, and a higher level of happiness. It will teach you how to manage life's challenges and downs with ease and grit, enhancing the path to self-actualization and your personal development. Take part in this insightful journey into mindfulness. This adventure promises to awaken your senses, widen your perspective, and provide participants with techniques to live more consciously as well as joyfully and fully.

THE ESSENCE OF MINDFULNESS AND ITS SIGNIFICANT ROLE IN DBT AND MENTAL HEALTH

To comprehend the significance that mindfulness has in promoting mental well-being It's important to be aware of its purpose and the essence. The well-known Buddhist monk Thich Nhat Hanh, encapsulates mindfulness with the words "The present moment is the only time over which we have dominion." The statement outlines the essential aspect of mindfulness, which is an conscious act of anchoring yourself within the present, without judgement. In mindfulness, your focus is on 'now' and 'now' while paying attention to your feelings, thoughts and the world around you while they are unfolding as they happen in real-time.

At its beginning, mindfulness was an integral component of the ancient Eastern philosophical system of Buddhism. It was particularly associated with the notion of 'sati', the term used to define the continuous consciousness of the world around us. Although it has roots in the spiritual realm it has successfully moved into a variety of secular settings particularly the realm of mental health. In this field, it's used as an essential tool for therapeutic methods such as DBT.

The doctrines of Buddha stress the importance of mindfulness as a lens by which we see life and manage its many different complexity. The majority of our personal issues are a result of personal issues that stem from feelings of self-worthlessness, insecurity and a deep sense of isolation. This personal, deeply embedded emotions may weaken our intrinsic resilience essential for our mental health. Understanding that, DBT incorporates mindfulness as an essential component of its therapeutic model.

Mindfulness is an essential ability within DBT that provides a strong foundation on which all others DBT techniques--distress tolerance and emotion control, and interpersonal efficiency are developed.

According to the understanding of DBT mindfulness is comprised of two essential elements: acceptance and awareness. Awareness is the conscious concentration on the present moment of our thoughts, feelings and bodily sensations when they take place, while being observant of them without modifying or removing their reality. constitute. Being present is about being a witness to our own experience.

However, acceptance is rooted deeply in the Buddhist doctrine and The Four Noble Truths, which affirms that our lusts and misunderstandings lie fundamental to suffering. Simply put our lives are often subjected to suffering by putting negative interpretations of our experience. However, if we be able to see these influences in a non-judgmental manner--which is the very essence of accepting them--we'll be able to better manage the negative feelings as well as the subsequent reaction they provoke. Mindfulness is the exact opposite of mindlessness. It is an attitude in which events are ignored, brushed aside and relegated to the background. It is often used as an excuse to avoid.

Mindfulness practices, when integrated in DBT can bring many advantages. They improve the effectiveness of the techniques taught in DBT and can help reduce the stress levels that people taking part in DBT could feel. Evidence-based research suggests that the integration of mindfulness-based elements into DBT will significantly improve the quality of life for clients and psychological wellbeing overall.

Furthermore, mindfulness has also been demonstrated to enhance the longevity of DBT. It is clear that the benefits of mindfulness goes beyond the realm of sessions with therapists, the benefits of mindfulness influencing all areas of people's lives. It could lead to improved capacity to deal with anxiety, improved emotional control as well as better relationships with others and an overall rise in capacity to be able to fully engage and appreciate completely with the present moment. So, mindfulness within DBT is a valuable technique for coping within the therapy space as well as a skill for life that patients can take with them when they embark on their path to recovering from mental illness.

THE TRANSFORMATIVE POWER OF MINDFULNESS IN REGULATING AND STABILIZING EMOTIONS

Much like a turbulent river our feelings can pull us into an array of directions, creating swirls of chaos that could overtake our lives. The emotional currents' overwhelming intensity can seem overwhelming, the resulting effects are unpredicted and devasting. With the aid of meditation, we possess the ability to change our position from reluctant participants in this tidal wave of emotion into calm, observant observers on the edge of the river. When we are mindful it helps us develop the capacity to look at the fluctuation and the flow of our emotions in a state of peaceful acceptance, without getting caught the turbulence, but calmly acknowledging their existence as they pass.

Through consistent practice of mindfulness We increase our ability to control our emotional environment and become less receptive to triggers that cause impulsive emotional reactions. The transformative effect of mindfulness is clearly demonstrated through the life of Karla and Rodney. The couple sought out counseling following a decision to divorce after five years of marriage after a string of emotional problems, such as the birth trauma of Karla and her subsequent postpartum mental illness, and Rodney's feelings of abandonment in the midst of his struggle to cope with the new paternal duties.

At the beginning of our sessions with counsellors, Karla's heightened anxiety levels caused a blockage preventing her from engaging effectively in our discussions. It was an instance of obvious regression, when Karla abruptly quit the session. This indicated that she was struggling with her anxiety. The path towards recovery from trauma slowly unfolded and she started to feel more at ease.

Over time, Karla developed a newfound view of herself, realizing that the condition of her mind does not determine her value. The realization helped her consider her disorder as an identifying factor, instead of a hinderance. Therefore, she decided to engage with positive activities such as journaling. This effectively diverted her attention away of negative feelings and altering her mental outlook.

We also taught mindfulness to Rodney and helped him develop empathy and compassion, which are crucial abilities for his relationships with Karla and their baby. The impact of mindfulness quickly became visible in the behavior of Rodney. He was able to be able to sympathize with the challenges of Karla as well as care for their baby and control his reaction to the events of Karla more calmly and kindly. Instead of reacting in a rash manner He learned to react calmly, giving his support, without absorbing her emotions.

While the couple continued to travel mindfully, they noticed an incremental but profound change in the dynamics of their relationships. The frequently intense and frequent emotional storms were able to calm down but when they came up they were handled by embracing grace and resiliency. The mindfulness practices they practiced became an intimate sanctuary and a refuge that allowed them to feel at peace as well as reconnect and strengthen the bonds they shared despite their emotional struggle.

Though it's not the solution for the entirety of their problems the practice of mindfulness was an empowerment tool, allowing individuals to tackle their anxieties and challenges together, changing their relationships and lives.

Through the stories from Karla and Rodney and Rodney, it is clear that mindfulness provides us with the key to our natural capacity to control our emotional state. This helps us recognize that emotions can be temporary They are fleeting and don't have the power to determine the way we behave or define our identity. Instead of viewing the emotions of our lives as a daunting obstacle instead, we should view them as useful tools that provide insight into our mind's internal functions. When we treat our emotions in a manner that is compassionate, gentle and a calm, peaceful acceptance you build up your emotional resilience and empower ourselves to manage the ups and downs of life better.

Additionally, as we expand our knowledge and develop mindfulness, we develop the ability to be able to see our emotions with no judgement. This creates the space to feel our emotions completely without becoming overwhelmed. This can bring about radical changes in our relationship with others and ourselves and allows for greater understanding of compassion and understanding of others' and our feelings. The complexities of our emotions by gaining more peace and control leading to better, healthier and happier lives.

ADDRESSING DIMINISHED AWARENESS, SELF-CONFUSION, AND IMPAIRED FOCUS

What is the reason it's an issue for the majority of us to concentrate on our work or goals particularly when it demands to be fully aware of the present current moment? The only way to do this is to keep our focus only for a few minutes before giving in to boredom anger, discontent, or distracted. If this goes on it can make us feel disoriented, frustrated and disengaged. Certain people experience little irritations seem to make their moods go into spiral. Others, the problem is to understand how they feel during certain scenarios.

Our minds are just like bakers that must be constantly focused on their work. But, when an abundance of tasks and people competing for our attention then we lose our focus and could lose our focus. It could be due to external factors, stressors or information overload as well as internal causes like fatigue or mental physical health issues, loss of self-awareness, confusion and a loss of focus are harmful to our professional relationships, as well as overall health.

Now, imagine this scenario it's 3:00pm - one hour prior to a major event. It's time to brainstorm three ideas to tackle the topic but you're difficult to stay focused. And, worse of all you're feeling stomach pains as you've received a message from a colleague about your friend that was arrested for drunk driving earlier in the night. This is an enormous strain on the mental well-being of your family as you're totally disoriented.

Although it seems like there are a variety of external causes that are to blame however what's really at fault is your mental state in all of the confusion. While we'd love to avoid unpleasant events it's not like a comedy show in which everything runs smoothly. Events that aren't expected pop up frequently. It's about recognizing these events and knowing how to manage these situations.

Interpreting and understanding situations is an actual struggle when we lack awareness or even a little. This is because our judgement and perception skills are thrown completely out of the window. In this situation you're unable to hold important conversations, take intelligent choices, or be able to absorb details. The self-confused, in contrast could cause us be unsure of our identity and goals or even our purpose and can be a trigger for anxiety and stress.

Although these challenges to cognitive functioning can be solved with simple steps However, sometimes the solution may involve just scratching at the surface to identify the underlying reason. As an example, problems with cognitive function can be caused by medical issues such as dementia, Alzheimer's trauma to the brain, as well as neurological diseases. Patients with these illnesses could suffer from:

Increased forgetfulness, particularly in recalling events from the past or conversations

Trouble concentrating on tasks

The confusion is based on the time, location or the familiar surroundings

Disorientation or mental fog

You are struggling to follow the instructions or follow directions

There is a higher chance of losing items

Separation from their thinking or their actions

Inability to take choices or resolve difficulties

Having difficulty in expressing themselves in a clear manner

In the situation mentioned previously it is possible that the fear of hearing about the arrest of a partner and fear of not being able to make the test could result in panic attacks. The symptoms mentioned above could be present even without existing ailments.

What can be done to combat this inability to concentrate? First, we need to identify the medical conditions that may be underlying and require the assistance of a professional. For instance, conditions like dementia or Alzheimer's are diagnosed and controlled with the help of medication or psychotherapy. When there's no treatment practices, mindfulness methods are a way to increase memory, self-awareness as well as focus (more on this subject in the final section of this section).

The choices we make in our lives also matter. In particular, regular exercise is a great way to improve brain blood flow and boost neuroplasticity. Foods must be of an abundance of nutrients to improve the memory and learning. This is particularly true for the nutrients that aid in the health of our brains, like omega-3 acid, antioxidants as well as B vitamin. It is also essential to have minimum seven hours of sleep each evening to ensure that we are functioning well and consolidation of memory. If we're not getting enough sleep it is important to engage in physically stimulating pursuits, keep track of the level of stress, and ensure that we maintain healthy social networks.

CORE SKILLS IN MINDFULNESS: OBSERVE, DESCRIBE, AND PARTICIPATE

When practicing mindfulness, there's a handful of core competencies that can help people develop a greater sense of being aware and present within the present. Some of these are "observe," "describe," and "participate." We'll explore the three skills in greater detail to discover their importance and use in daily living.

OBSERVE

The practice of observation is the foundation for meditation. It's a way of disciplining the mind and trains it to be attentive to the present moment using an attitude of non-reactivity being curious, and open. It is essentially the act of "observe" requires you to pay attention to all aspects of our outer and inner environments, from emotions and thoughts to physical sensations, and then into our interaction with the outside world.

Imagine sitting at the edge of an immense forest and preparing for the journey of discovery. Through mindfulness, this vast nature is a reflection of the depths of both our internal and external encounters. A practice of "observing" is the initial step in the woods, and it is where we are consciously deciding to investigate and comprehend our surroundings without preconceived beliefs or opinions.

The most important thing to do is to adopt a mindset that is non-reactive. Instead of becoming entangled in emotions, thoughts or feelings as they come up We learn to observe these as unbiased observer. Let them come and go, without trying to limit, silence or attach to the feelings. In the case, for example, when the feelings of anxiety start to arise and we are unable to dispel them or getting caught up in worrying thoughts, we just look at them as they occur - observing their presence but not responding to the feelings.

A third and crucial aspect of observation is the pursuit of curiosity. Our approach to our observations is by having an open and curious mind, ready to look at any possibility that arises, without judgement. It's not a passive observer rather an active participation in the present moment with curiosity and understanding. If it's a brief moment of sensation, an ongoing thinking pattern, or even a delicate sensation within the body We explore it by observing it with awe. We don't label it as good or 'bad', but instead accepting its existence.

Practically speaking, it is as simple as taking note of the feeling of your breath rushing through your body and out, noting the feel of air against your skin as well as observing the flow of thoughts when dealing with a stressful circumstance. Once we have developed this ability it becomes easier to spot small details we may had previously missed - such as our changing thinking, the shifting and the flow of our emotions as well as the interaction of different the sensory experience we have in our surroundings.

The act of "observing" is also applicable to our outside world. It is a way to become conscious and focused when we interact with people as well as our daily activities. It can turn everyday activities into moments of mindful awareness in which washing dishes can be an opportunity to experience the warm sensation or having a chat with a person is a time to pay attention to their thoughts, emotions as well as their perspective.

How can we apply this to our lives? Here are some suggestions:

Take note of your breath. It is important to observe the rhythm of your breathing when you exhale and inhale. Simply observe the pattern without trying to alter the pattern. This is an easy and effective way of establishing you in the present.

Listen to the music: Take note of the noises around you or as a unit. Pay attention to the distinctive features of each one and the way it affects your surroundings. It's a great way to become more aware of your surroundings and increase your awareness.

Let your thoughts flow past: Instead of getting immersed in the flow of thoughts, just observe them as they go and disappear. You don't have to follow them, or even judge their movements, instead let them drift by like clouds on the sky. This encourages detachment and lets you choose the direction you want to put your focus.

Pay attention to your body as well as the surrounding environment: Pay attention to the physical sensations you feel and your surroundings. Be aware of the sensory sensations that you feel in your body as well as the scents, textures as well as the hues of your surroundings. This helps to stay moment and increases your overall awareness.

DESCRIBE

Beyond observational merely"describe the experience' requires an extra dimension of conscious engagement. The mindfulness aspect sharpens our ability to see by encouraging us to frame the experiences we encounter. The essence of 'describe' refers to defining and explaining our experiences, both internal and external in a precise and objective manner, making abstract concepts concrete and definable components.

Think of our minds as huge areas of uncharted territory. This process of observation permits the mind to get a better understanding of this world as well, and the act of "describe" is similar to drawing a precise sketch of the things we see. It is possible to identify particular locations (emotions or thoughts) and note their specific characteristics and clearly articulate them.

The process involves separating the raw information that we receive from our sensations and the actual reality of the situationas well as the emotional reactions and interpretations that they trigger within us. When it comes to this, identifying the experiences we experience and how they are expressed is essential.

Let's take an example: you're worried about your coming speech. Instead of categorizing the entire scenario in terms of "stressful," which is unclear and carries negative connotations, recognize the particular sensations that are that are associated with anxiety, such as the rumbling of your body, sweaty hands and a nagging worry about the possibility of loss. A detailed explanation helps you make your experience more concrete to make them more manageable and less stressful.

It's not unusual for individuals to mistake their emotions as stimuli from outside. The confusion can be exacerbated and create a challenge to come up with a suitable response. In the example above, a person might think that a heart race is the sign of a imminent medical crisis, but it could be simply an expression of anxiety idea.

In learning to differentiate emotions from a factual situation, we can gain a better perception of what we are experiencing. Then we step away from our emotional responses and evaluate them in perspective of factual information. This method of "describe" lets us look at the experiences we experience from a independent and objective viewpoint and improves our capacity to manage the complexities of life with calmness and wisdom.

Writing down our experience is essential to convey our emotions effectively to other people. When we're able to articulate clearly the inner turmoil we experience We are more able to communicate our desires and limits, thereby fostering better interpersonal relationships.

How can effectively describe what we have experienced?

Don't make judgments Be careful not to be judgmental in describing your experiences may cloud our judgment and cause us to drift off from an objective perspective. If, for instance, we are feeling unloved It is important to acknowledge the feeling as untrue and subjective. It's not a representation of reality.

Do not label with judgement labels can hinder the scope of our thinking and can create an unchanging perspective. Maybe you've heard phrases such as "I'm not creative" in specific situations. Like seeds, set the stage in preventing any effort to improve your skills create ideas and make the most of opportunities. This causes stagnation and low productivity.

Instead of stating "I'm not creative," it is better to be more observant and open way of thinking. You. might reframe the statement to read, "I notice that my thoughts and ideas are flowing less freely than usual." This change in terminology lets you describe your feelings without having to cling to rigid judgements.

Let's see how your writing skills is able to be a huge asset in many circumstances. Consider the following scenario situation: You are nearing the threshold of an deserved promotion. your boss asks you to the task of presenting an idea for an internal initiative. In a state of inspiration You come up with bunch of ideas, and you're determined to communicate them to your coworker for feedback. But, your colleague is distracted by other work that he's been unable to provide your idea the respect it is due.

This naturally demoralizes and demoralizes. What would be the reaction you have to his absence?

A) "My ideas suck!"

(b) "My colleague isn't very enthusiastic about my ideas."

C) "I feel like my colleague envies my promotion and so can't support me."

"D") "It seems like my coworker is entangled in a plethora of things currently. Maybe I'll be able to pitch my thoughts to him in the future."

Which is more a statement of reality (truth)? Of course, D. On the contrary, choices A, B and C have to do with emotions.

PARTICIPATE

"Realize deeply that the present moment is all you ever have," philosopher Eckhart Tolle famously advised. The aphorism perfectly explains the notion of participation, a crucial skill for meditation. Participation is the act of stepping in to the present moment completely embracing each event as it unfolds. It's the most active aspect of mindfulness that bridges the space between action and observation.

Being in a time full of constant interruptions, it's easy to live our lives in a loop, cruising through the days, our thoughts wandering off to other places, unable to focus on actual reality in the moment. While this apathy might seem innocent, it could have a profound impact. It can lead to frequent mistakes and misjudgments. It also blocks our minds from the depth of our lives, limiting the ability of us to truly engage with our surroundings and each other. Take a look at the many times you've used words like "I'm sorry, I didn't think it through," or "I'm sorry, it just happened." Although these phrases may appear to be genuine excuses for mistakes but they highlight a crucial problem - - the lack of awareness in the present moment. In ignoring the instantaneity of our lives and experiences, we lose the opportunity to truly connect, understand as well as personal development.

The act of participation, when viewed in an environment of mindful confronts this autopilot way of lifestyle. It prompts us to switch off our autopilot function and to actively participate in the world around us. This isn't just about performing things, but soaking ourselves into the experience, taking in the nuances of every moment.

Participation in the real world can take on different forms -being fully engaged in a conversation with your loved one and savoring every bite of food and tackling an activity with passion and intensity. Each event offers the chance to be fully involved, and a full of the present.

It also includes our emotions. Instead of shunning unpleasant emotions, or holding onto positive ones, we are taught to be present in these emotions, embracing their presence and managing their nuance through empathy and understanding. When we do this it allows us to create an emotional world that is marked by compassion of, acceptance, and the ability to endure.

In addition, participating in mindfulness helps us connect to our own inner self. Through active participation in every minute, we improve the awareness of ourselves, and develop greater awareness of our emotions, thoughts and actions. The increased self-awareness serves as an opportunity to grow personally and improvement, which contributes to our overall wellbeing.

By focusing on our participation and mindful participation, we can help bridge this gap. Here's the way:

It is important to learn how to tackle routine tasks with new perspective. Instead of saying "This is boring," take a deep dive into the task by observing it and then imagining the experience to yourself. As an example, if you're a logistics professional who unloads and loads shipments often, you must be immersed when you're working. Beware of labels that make you feel like, "I really hate this job" or "It's just a waste of time." Instead focus your attention on machines' sounds, complex packaging that accompanies the shipment and the sensations of touch while your legs and arms effortlessly shift from one place in one place to another, and all else that serves as a the purpose it has.

Don't be afraid to allow yourself to doubt. It's easy to fall in the trap of self-deceit, and make excuses to justify our actions, particularly if it seems like we've been put down the road. A conscious participation allows us to assume complete responsibility for our actions, by understanding what's really happening as well as making a fair and objective evaluation.

Be aware of every emotion whether it's a pleasant one or not. While doing this, make sure you stick to facts and not be lost in your emotions.

PRACTICAL EXERCISES AND EXAMPLES OF ENHANCING MINDFULNESS

Understanding what mindfulness means and how it could apply to our daily life doesn't suffice and we must adopt the more methodical approach and apply it effectively. Take a moment to think about the last time you found yourself faced with a dilemma that needed taking a decision, whether either personal or professional. Did you think about how much time and thought you consider the issue prior to making a decision? The answer you give is an excellent indication of how attentive you considered your decision.

I've put together some simple techniques to assist you in implementing mindfulness into your everyday routine:

OBSERVE

The exercise involves focusing on a specific object for five minutes. This is recommended to repeat it 3 times in a week.

Step One: Find a Comfortable Space

Your space for mind training is supposed to be peaceful and free of clutter to avoid distractions. After you've checked those boxes then settle down. Breathe deeply and then let go of the breath slowly so that the muscles relax. Repeat this process until you're comfortable.

Step Two: Select an Object and Focus on It

This can be any tiny gadget you utilize every day including a notepad, a pencil or an Rubik's cube. No matter what you choose, be sure that the item does not have an significance for you emotionally. Don't pick one that brings back memories of someone else you've loved or grandmother's birthday because this could prove emotional.

Take note of the object using all your senses, for around five minutes. Be aware of the size as well as its color, shape as well as texture and even its weight. How does it feel inside your hands? What does it sound like when you touch it? Do you notice a distinct scent?

It's common for the mind to wander when you're doing this. It's possible to start thinking about the meeting scheduled at around 3.00 p.m. or your gym membership expiring sometime later during the morning. If this occurs it is a good idea to gently direct your attention towards your goal and keep your focus.

Step Three: Notice and Accept Your Internal Experiences

It is possible to react to the workout in different ways such as feeling bored, confused or even exuberant. This is perfectly normal. You shouldn't dismiss or judge any personal experience or place your opinion on the event. It is important to simply observe and write down what you observe without prejudice. This may be uncomfortable at first, but in time your ability to stay focussed and objective will affect the outcome of your choices.

Step Four: Document Your Experience

After the task, record the experience you have had. It is a good idea to use a worksheet to record this. Note the time, date, what you was observed, its characteristics as well as the emotions the item evoked. This can help you record the improvements that you've achieved. Even if you don't feel you've improved, don't fret. Like any technique, it takes practice to become the perfect.

MENTAL BODY SCAN

The exercise involves scanning your body for fifteen minutes. This should be completed each day throughout the week.

Choose a comfy sitting seat in a chair and place your feet on the ground or cushions. Take a deep breath, then breathe deeply to calm yourself.

The first step is to bring your focus to your lower body. Focus initially on your feet. Notice any sensations or emotions below. Are they cool or warm? Are you feeling some tingling or tension? Be aware and not judge.

Then slowly move your attention towards your lower thighs and knees. Take note of any sensations, like tension or relaxation. Pay especially attention to those areas which might feel tight or stiff.

Then, bring your attention towards your legs, especially the upper your hips. Be aware of your body's weight being supported by your cushion or chair. Feel any sensations you feel around this part of your body that indicate weight or a sense of lightness.

Focus your attention on your lower back and abdomen and note any discomforts you feel there, as well as the way your lower back is in contact with your chair.

Then, bring your attention towards your upper body beginning with your chest, and back. Feel any sensations that you can feel throughout these parts while you breathe. You can feel the expanding and contracting of your chest as you take every breath.

You can focus your attention upwards towards your neck and shoulders. Be aware of any tightness or tension around this region.

As you breathe, try the release of tension, allow your shoulders to relax and loosen your neck.

Then, turn your focus to your head and your face. Pay attention to any sensations, like the sensation of warmth or cooling. Look for any tension on your jaw, forehead or temples. Try to let these areas relax and allow your jaw to become more relaxed and your jaw to loosen.

If you're feeling ready take a moment to open your eyes and then take a few moments for a transition to the world around you.

MINDFUL BREATHING

There are three kinds of breathing exercises: counting breaths, observing the effects of breathing, and diaphragmatic breathing.

Counting Breaths

Choose a calm and comfortable spot to relax or lay down. If you're sitting, place your body in a relaxed position with your back straight and relax shoulders.

Close your eyes and take a few slow breaths, allowing yourself to fall to a peaceful state.

It is best to begin by watching your breathing, without interrupting. Take note of the rhythmic nature of your breathing along with the fluctuating feeling in your body and also the motion of your chest or abdomen.

When you are able to focus in your breathing, you can begin to count every breath cycle. A whole breath cycle comprises of an inhale and an exhale.

Take a deep, slow inhale through your nose. Then, when you exhale out of your mouth begin to count "one." Inhale again then exhale and count "two." Continue this repetition, counting each breath until you have reached the number "10."

Once you've reached the number 10 begin again starting from a new number. If you are unable to count, or your thoughts begin to wander, just be aware of this and get your mind back on your breath and counting.

Repeat the counting process starting at one, and ending at 10. Repeat this counting cycle for several minutes, or for as long as you'd prefer. Relax and let your breath become your focus without letting go of any distracting thoughts or ideas.

After you've completed the activity, observe any changes as you write your experiences.

Noting the Sensations of Breathing

You should find a comfortable place such as lying or sitting down. Ensure the body remains at ease and straight.

Shut your eyes and breathe deeply to relax and center yourself.

Focus your attention on the physical sensations that accompany breathing. Be aware of the cooling air that is drawn into your nose as well as the warm breath as you exhale. Be aware of the way your body is moving with each breath.

Focus your attention on the movement of your stomach as well as the contraction and expansion of the chest. Be aware of the movements that are gentle as well as how they relate to the breath you take.

Pay attention to the sensation of air coming into and exiting your nostrils. Be aware of the sensations that come from the breath while it travels through the nostrils.

Pay attention to subtle shifts in your body while you breath. Pay attention to the tension or relaxation with each breath and exhalation. Keep an eye on the pace and rhythm of your breath.

If you notice your mind drifts or thoughts come up be sure to acknowledge them with no judgement and then shift your focus to the feelings of breathing.

Keep observing and feel the physical sensations that come from breathing for several minutes. Take the time to completely immerse yourself into the sensation.

If you're ready to end the workout (after approximately 10 minutes) Take a few deep breaths. Then, slowly re-awaken the awareness of your surroundings then slowly open your eyes.

Note down any experiences and improvements you've observed.

Diaphragmatic Breathing

Relaxation techniques, such as deep breathing or called deep or belly breathing can help reduce stress, relax the mind, and create an overall sense of wellbeing. This is how you can do it:

Choose a comfy spot. It is possible to sit in a chair and place your feet laying flat on the floor or lie on your back, with your legs a little apart, and the arms resting at your side.

Shut your eyes and then take a few minutes to be in tune with the body as well as your breathing. Be aware of any discomfort or tension as you allow yourself to ease into a state of relaxation.

You can place one hand on your chest, and another hand resting placed on your stomach close to the ribcage. It will allow you to be conscious of the movements that your breath makes.

Take a slow and deep breath with your nose. Allow the air to be absorbed into your abdominal. You will feel your stomach increase as it is filled with air. Keep your chest relaxed.

After exhaling take a few seconds to release breath from your mouth discovering your stomach sinking downwards. Feel the sensation of your air disappearing from your body.

Keep this practice going by concentrating on the motion of your abdominal muscles. Take a deep breath, allowing your stomach to raise while exhaling slowly, being aware of the fall. Breath slowly easy, natural, and smooth.

When you breathe, release yourself from any distractions or thoughts to focus solely on the experience of your breathing and the motion of your abdomen. If you feel your mind has been wandering, slowly bring the focus to your breathing.

DESCRIBE

Step One: Select an Emotion

The method focuses on feelings and feelings, so begin by looking at the way you're feeling this moment, regardless of whether you feel good, bad or disgusting. If you're experiencing feelings that are too overwhelming, consider what you've experienced recently and find it easier to deal with. Perhaps you're thinking about an unpleasant working day or exciting adventure you had with your favorite loved one. Note the feelings generated - be it emotion of excitement, anger or anger. For the sake of making it easier make two lists of your emotions, categorized in the category of "positive" and "negative."

Step Two: Paint a Picture of the Emotion

It's the time to let loose your self-defence Leonardo Da Vinci, even if you're not a professional artist. Draw what your emotions appear as in a style that resonates with your. In the case of example, if you're feeling happy and happy, draw a colorful butterfly to express your feelings.

Step 3: Choose the Action That Matches Your Feeling

Think of an action that is exactly to your current emotions. If you are being excited, it might be beneficial to note down phrases like "freedom," "happy," or "vibrant." This will help you to express how the feeling resonates in you.

Step Four: Express the Intensity of Your Emotion

You can rate your feelings using a scale from 10 to 0 where 10 is the most intense emotion. You can also come up with your own expressions such as "tough as nails," "angry as a bull," or "happy as a clam" to express the emotion.

Step Five: Record the thoughts that result from the emotional state

Jot down any ideas you get during the exercise. Make sure that these thoughts are just ideas rather than emotions. Also, avoid employing words from the list you've made previously. Imagine you're happy over a night out you had. This could lead to an urge to have another enjoyable excursion. If you're unhappy You might consider relaxing.

Chapter 10: Cultivating Resilience Through Distress Tolerance

In all of its uncertainty and the complexities of life, there are certain moments of sadness. It doesn't matter if it's pressure from obligations to study, the pressures of working in a profession and the challenges of family relationships, or anxieties regarding financial stability All of us face difficulties which, in some instances, can leave us feeling stressed and nervous. When we are in these situations the ability we have to handle stress and demonstrate the characteristic I call "stress resilience" truly makes the difference. The ability to master distress tolerance, or the capacity to endure and manage stressful circumstances without slipping into emotional chaos can be a valuable ability that opens the door to optimal health and personal development.

In this section we'll dive deeper into the notion of stress tolerance and its importance in the journey to better wellbeing and mental well-being. I'll discuss strategies, methods as well as insights that I have used personally to guide me through difficult times. These tools aren't only dealing with the devastation of despair, they are created to improve your emotional, physical and spiritual health.

The first step is to understand distress from an overall perspective and explore its causes as well as its impact on our lives and our common responses to distress. On this basis will be a discussion of the value of resilience to distress and explain the reasons why resilience, and not avoidance, leads to an energizing and healthy living.

The next step is to explore the various methods and strategies that are designed for enhancing your stress tolerance. These methods will not only provide you with the necessary techniques for dealing with difficult times however, they will help you develop understanding more deeply your personal emotional environment. There will be discussions on mindfulness and cognitive reframing strategies as well as self-soothing techniques as well as other techniques designed to provide you with a the most effective tools to manage anxiety.

In the closing portion of this chapter we'll examine the importance of self-care for resilience to distress. In this section, we'll emphasize the importance of well-being, emotional self-awareness and spiritual nourishment for maintaining the balance and resilience during times in distress. The comprehensive method ensures you're not just living through times of stress however, you're flourishing.

Be aware that distress tolerance isn't focused on eliminating stress out of our lives. That's an unattainable goal. It's more about cultivating the ability to endure the waves of life in a calm and confident manner as well as using the moments as opportunities to develop. When you're through this section, I'm hoping that you'll increase your ability to face life's challenges not with survival only at the forefront, but also with a the goal of health as well as personal growth as the primary focus.

Let's begin with the basics.

THE CONCEPT OF DISTRESS AND ITS EFFECT ON MENTAL AND PHYSICAL HEALTH

It's a term that encompasses a variety of feelings and emotions which range from feeling in a state of disarray to suffering from severe suffering, or simply being in an acute state of anxiety. The state of distress is not one that most one would prefer to choose however, many of us encounter it in the depths of it because of a variety of stresses or events in our lives. They could be anything from constant tension, painful situations, financial troubles or relationship problems as well as major changes in our lives.

The concept of distress in the way we understand it in the present, has its origins to Hans Selye's General Adaptation Syndrome (GAS) theory. GAS describes a series of mental and physical reactions that occur when we are confronted with stressful or dangerous conditions. This can involve a struggle to deal with stress, leading to anxiety. Sometimes, stress may trigger positive reactions that create a feeling of enthusiasm and energy which is known as stress.

In the beginning, people viewed distress as an internal tension that was caused by stressors external to us. However, this perception has been enhanced through the research that psychology professor Richard Lazarus, who proposed that our responses to stress reflect the dynamic interaction between ourselves as well as our surroundings. In this way, stress is a sign of our struggle to adapt to the demands of our environment.

Think about a scenario in which the workload of your business suddenly increases by 50percent. It is not surprising that you may feel depressed when this sudden change pushes you to the edge of the limits of your experience and abilities. With the added pressures placed upon you could strain you so thin that they hinder the efficiency and productivity of your work. Why? because your capabilities do not match up with the expectations set for you.

The negative effects of stress in our general wellbeing are well documented The most dangerous effects result from exposure to stress that is chronic. If we are confronted by an extreme stressor our bodies trigger an hormonal cascade that primes the brain as well as various organs to ward off any perceived danger. The "fight or flight" response raises blood pressure, speeds up the rate of heartbeat, and increases the strength of our immune system. It floods the body with white blood cells as well as additional natural defenses.

But, when the initial surge of hormones recedes the physiological alterations that are triggered may be detrimental, especially when the stress response is repeatedly activated. Continuously elevated levels of stress hormones can hinder the relaxing of our blood vessels, and alters the ability of our heart to pump blood. This results in increased blood pressure and raises the chance of developing cardiovascular disease which include heart attacks.

In addition, stress hormones may affect the function of brain neurons which are involved in memory, learning and processing of emotions. These disruptions can hinder cognition, which can lead to confusion and forgetfulness. In extreme instances, intense stress levels or long periods of stress could lead to irreparable brain injury.

www.ingramcontent.com/pod-product-compliance
Lightning Source LLC
Chambersburg PA
CBHW051726020426
42333CB00014B/1170